Combat Aircraft Library

American
Fighters
of World War II

David A. Anderton

Crescent Books
New York

Crescent Books

First English edition published 1982 by
The Hamlyn Publishing Group Limited, and now
published by Temple Press an imprint of Newnes Books

Printed and bound in Italy

Created and produced by Stan Morse
Aerospace Publishing Ltd
10 Barley Mow Passage
London W4 4PH

All correspondence concerning the content of this volume should be addressed to Aerospace
Publishing Limited. Trade enquiries should be addressed to Crescent Books, New York.

ISBN: 0-517-37482X

Library of Congress Catalogue Card Number: 83-70 129

PICTURE ACKNOWLEDGEMENTS

The publishers would like to thank the following people and organisations listed below for their
help in supplying photographs for this book.

Jacket front: US Air Force. **Jacket back:** John MacClancy. **Page 1:** John MacClancy.
5: Grumman Aircraft Corporation. **6:** (top) US Air Force. **7:** US Navy. **14:** US Air Force/
US Navy. **17:** US Air Force. **18:** (bottom) John MacClancy. **19:** US Air Force. **24/25:** John
MacClancy. **27:** John MacClancy. **32:** (bottom) US Air Force. **33:** US Air Force. **34:** US Air
Force. **40:** US Navy. **41:** US Navy. **42:** US Navy. **43:** US Navy/US Navy. **44:** US Navy/US Navy.
45: US Navy/US Navy. **49:** John MacClancy. **50:** Vought Corporation/Vought Corporation.
51: Vought Corporation. **52:** US Navy/US Navy. **52:** US Navy/US Navy. **56:** US Navy.
58: US Navy/US Navy. **59:** US Navy/US Navy. **60:** Harold G. Martin. **61:** US Air Force.
69: US Air Force. **72:** US Air Force. **73:** North American. **74:** US Air Force. **76:** US Navy/
US Navy. **77:** US Navy.

Foreword

'The danger inherent in any report confined to one aspect of the war is that it may mislead the reader into forgetting that the conflict was won by a combination of ground, naval, and air forces. . .' So said the United States Navy's Vice Admiral Forrest Sherman in 1947, when he was Deputy Chief of Naval Operations, and it is worth keeping that in mind as we begin this survey of American fighters of World War II.

When war came, the fighter strength of the United States lagged behind those of its future allies and enemies. Its service aircraft were either obsolescent or at the end of their potential development. New types neared production, but a long and difficult period of maturing lay ahead before they could tangle with the enemy on anything but a very unequal footing. Armament was hardly better than it had been in World War I, and altitude performance, range, speed and manoeuvrability were generally poor.

By the end of the war, American designers had produced several fighter aircraft since recognized as classics. American production lines, untouched by the daily reality of war, enjoyed the twin luxuries of time and distance. Because of them, US factories were able to build an unequalled capacity that turned out fighting aircraft by the tens of thousands.

Without exception, though, the American fighters that helped wind up the long conflict had been ordered into development before war began for the United States. In some cases, the planes were in design before September 1939, when all Hell broke loose on the Polish border with Germany.

So here they are, a galaxy of American fighters. Some were classics, and some were clunkers. But—as part of a brave company—they helped to hold, and then to roll back, a fearsome, ruthless and cruel enemy.

Judge them on their merits, in the context of their times.

Contents

The First Round

The Americans had come up with some neat ideas in the 1930s. But the blooding of Europe in 1939 shows that these ideas had not been put together as the right packages.

Snarling Boeing P-26 pursuits, resplendent in blue bodies and chrome-yellow wings and tail.

Grumman aircraft were from the start so strong the company became known as 'The Ironworks'. Showing the patented retractable landing gear is an F3F-2.

The United States, before World War II, was a country that seemed to want only to live in splendid and impossible isolation from the rest of the world. It was secure behind friendly borders to the north and south, and protected by vast expanses of ocean to the east and west. With no plans of territorial expansion, or of attacking another country, America's security policy was one of defence.

The US Navy was the primary agent of that policy, assigned to defend the coasts in co-operation with strategically placed batteries of the US Army's Coast Artillery. The US Army itself was small, still largely equipped with the rifles, machine-guns, artillery and personal gear used in World War I.

Air power was a very subordinate arm of both major services. In the US Army, very limited availability of funding had forced some cruel choices, including a concentration on the bomber

Curtiss P-36

SPECIFICATION
Type: single-seat fighter
Powerplant: (P-36C) one 1,200-hp (895-kW) Pratt & Whitney R-1830-17 Twin Wasp radial piston engine
Performance: maximum speed 311 mph (501 km/h) at 10,000 ft (3050 m); cruising speed 270 mph (435 km/h); service ceiling 33,700 ft (10270 m); range 820 miles (1320 km)
Weights: empty 4,620 lb (2096 kg); maximum take-off 6,010 lb (2726 kg)
Dimensions: span 37 ft 4 in (11.38 m); length 28 ft 6 in (8.69 m); height 9 ft 6 in (2.90 m); wing area 236 sq ft (21.92 m²)
Armament: one 0.50-in (12.7-mm) and three 0.30-in (7.62-mm) machine-guns

Curtiss P-36A of the 79th Pursuit Squadron, 20th Pursuit Group, Moffett Field, California, November 1939.

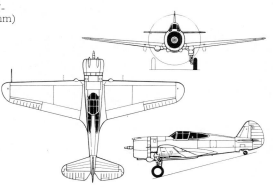

Curtiss P-36A (dotted wing guns show P-36C)

Curtiss P-36C of the 27th Pursuit Sqn, US Army Air Corps.

as the selected tool of the projection of air power. It made sense in light of the assumed security policy. Any attacker would have to invade, and would have to amass forces for that invasion. Bombers would seek out, attack and destroy the accumulation of ordnance, supplies and troops needed for such an invasion. No enemy aircraft capable of intercepting bombers so far from its own home bases was known to exist, and so it was assumed that the bombers would make their way to the target free of harassment. That assumption cost dearly over Europe, just a few years later.

The US Navy needed aircraft for scouting, and provision had been made long before 1939 for catapult operations of aircraft from cruisers and battleships. The five fleet carriers in commission were equipped with the very latest biplane fighters and bombers, and their mission was fleet defence.

The Boeing F4B-3 was one of the first fighters in the world to have a semi-monocoque stressed-skin fuselage. Three are seen after being passed from Navy fighter squadron VF-1B to shore service with the Marines.

Grumman F4F Wildcat

SPECIFICATION
Type: single-seat carrier-based fighter bomber
Powerplant: (F4F-4) one 1,200-hp (895-kW) Pratt & Whitney R-1830-86 Twin Wasp radial piston engine
Performance: maximum speed 318 mph (512 km/h) at 19,400 ft (5914 m); cruising speed 155 mph (249 km/h); service ceiling 39,400 ft (12010 m); range 770 miles (1239 km)
Weights: empty 5,758 lb (2612 kg); maximum take-off 7,952 lb (3607 kg)
Dimensions: span 38 ft 0 in (11.58 m); length 28 ft 9 in (8.76 m); height 9 ft 2½ in (2.81 m); wing area 260 sq ft (24.15 m²)
Armament: six 0.50-in (12.7mm) machine-guns and two 100-lb (45-kg) bombs

Grumman F4F-3 Wildcat of VF-7 aboard the USS Wasp, *December 1940.*

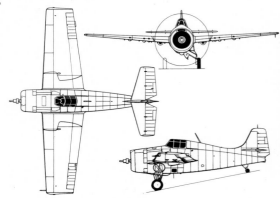

Grumman F4F Wildcat

Grumman F4F Wildcat aboard USS Santee *(ACV-29).*

In September 1939, the US Army Air Corps was equipped with a total of about 1,500 aircraft, of which 800 were claimed as first-line strength. The US Navy had a few more than 900 claimed as first-line, but several hundred of that number were obsolescent biplanes. Across the wide Atlantic, the Royal Air Force numbered about 2,000 first-line aircraft, plus reserves, and the Luftwaffe counted approximately 4,000 aircraft ready for combat, plus reserve strengths estimated as high as an additional 1,000. Personnel strength of the USAAC was less than 27,000 officers and men; that was about one-quarter of the RAF's strength, and one-twentieth of the Luftwaffe's personnel.

About 700 of the US Army's 800 first-line aircraft were three types: the standard fighter was the Curtiss P-36A, a graceful plane designed in 1934 and very near the end of its operational life; the standard bomber was the lumbering Douglas B-18A, a modified DC-3 with a

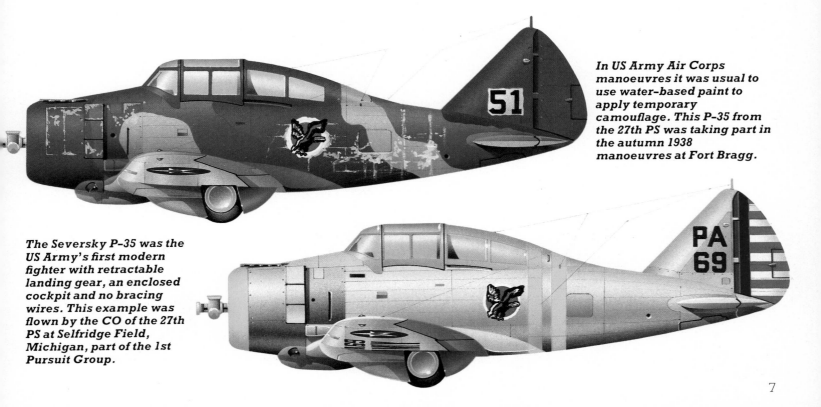

In US Army Air Corps manoeuvres it was usual to use water-based paint to apply temporary camouflage. This P-35 from the 27th PS was taking part in the autumn 1938 manoeuvres at Fort Bragg.

The Seversky P-35 was the US Army's first modern fighter with retractable landing gear, an enclosed cockpit and no bracing wires. This example was flown by the CO of the 27th PS at Selfridge Field, Michigan, part of the 1st Pursuit Group.

Curtiss P-36

Curtiss P-36A attached to the 35th Pursuit Sqn (Fighter) during 1939–40 while that unit was at Langley Field, Virginia and in transition to new quarters at Mitchell Field, New York.

The First Round

mis-shapen nose and a design that also dated back to 1934; and the standard attacker was the Northrop A-17A, a light two-seater that—after much later improvement and modification—eventually became the Douglas SBD, the US Navy's best bomber of the war.

The US Navy's first-line fighter in late 1939 was the stubby Grumman F3F, last of the biplane fighters in US service. Flown by US Marine Corps and US Navy pilots, the Grummans were based on four of the fleet carriers. Development of the US Navy's first monoplane fighter, the Brewster F2A, was under way, but that ill-fated craft was a long way from service, and had a dismal battle record when it finally did fight.

Lightning war in Europe

The rude awakening began in September 1939, with the frightening Blitzkrieg that slashed through Poland. It left behind a swath of destroyed cavalry units, obsolescent aircraft and defeated foot soldiers. The speed of the German advance, the combined use of air and ground forces, and the outstanding performance of the fledgling Luftwaffe—all amplified considerably by a very efficient propaganda machine—caused serious concern among the planners and builders of American defence industries.

Fortunately for the final outcome of the war, there had been a few determined backers of advanced fighters before the Germans made the need crystal clear. By the time the war began

Some fighter designers thought the XP–47B, first flown on 6 May 1941, a very mistaken answer to the fighter design problem, because of its size and weight. That did not stop the P–47 from becoming the most numerous US fighter in history.

in Europe, the USAAC had placed its first orders for the Lockheed P-38, the Bell P-39 and the Curtiss P-40. All had made their first flights before September 1939. The US Navy was receiving its first monoplane fighter, the Brewster F2A-1, and had ordered the rugged Grumman F4F-3 Wildcat into production. Both prototypes had flown during 1937. The experimental Vought XF4U-1, first of the 400-mph (645-km/h) class of fighters, had been ordered by mid-1938.

No longer in a front–line unit, these Bell P–39Ds are seen from an unusual angle at a training unit in 1942. The P–39 promised much in 1939, but proved to be very much an also–ran.

Between the launching of Germany's lightning war and the Japanese attack at Pearl Harbor, three additional aircraft entered the design process to become the most significant American fighters of the war. Republic's XP-47 began to take shape early in 1940. It was followed a few months later by every pilot's dream of a fighter, the North American NA-73, forerunner of the P-51 Mustang. On the US Navy side, Grumman's F6F Hellcat, slated to become the primary fighter in the Pacific theatre, was first defined by a simple request from the US Navy: put a

The First Round

For Operation 'Torch', the invasion of North Africa in November 1942, the Wildcat IIs (previously Martlet IIs) of Royal Navy No. 888 Sqn (HMS Formidable) were given US markings. Armed with six 0.5-in (12.7-mm) guns, this was the first model with folding wings.

Grumman F4F-4 Wildcat cutaway drawing key

1 Starboard navigation light
2 Wingtip
3 Starboard formation light
4 Rear spar
5 Aileron construction
6 Fixed aileron tab
7 All riveted wing construction
8 Lateral stiffeners
9 Forward canted main spar
10 'Crimped' leading edge ribs
11 Solid web forward ribs
12 Starboard outer gun blast tube
13 Carburettor air duct
14 Intake
15 Curtiss three-blade constant-speed propeller
16 Propeller cuffs
17 Propeller hub
18 Engine front face
19 Pressure baffle
20 Forward cowling ring
21 Cooler intake
22 Cooler air duct
23 Pratt & Whitney R-1830-86 radial engine
24 Rear cowling ring/flap support
25 Controllable cowling flaps
26 Downdraft ram air duct
27 Engine mounting ring
28 Anti-detonant regulator unit
29 Cartridge starter
30 Generator
31 Intercooler
32 Engine accessories
33 Bearer assembly welded cluster joint
34 Main beam
35 Lower cowl flap
36 Exhaust stub
37 Starboard mainwheel
38 Undercarriage fairing
39 Lower drag link
40 Hydraulic brake
41 Port mainwheel
42 Detachable hub cover
43 Low-pressure tyre
44 Axle forging
45 Upper drag link
46 Oleo shock strut
47 Ventral fairing
48 Wheel well
49 Pivot point
50 Landing light
51 Main forging
52 Compression link
53 Gun camera port
54 Counter balance
55 Anti-detonant tank
56 Retraction sprocket
57 Gear box
58 Stainless steel firewall
59 Engine bearers
60 Actuation chain (undercarriage)
61 Engine oil tank
62 Oil filler
63 Hoisting sling installation
64 Bullet resistant windscreen
65 Reflector gunsight
66 Panoramic rear-view mirror
67 Wing fold position
69 Adjustable headrest

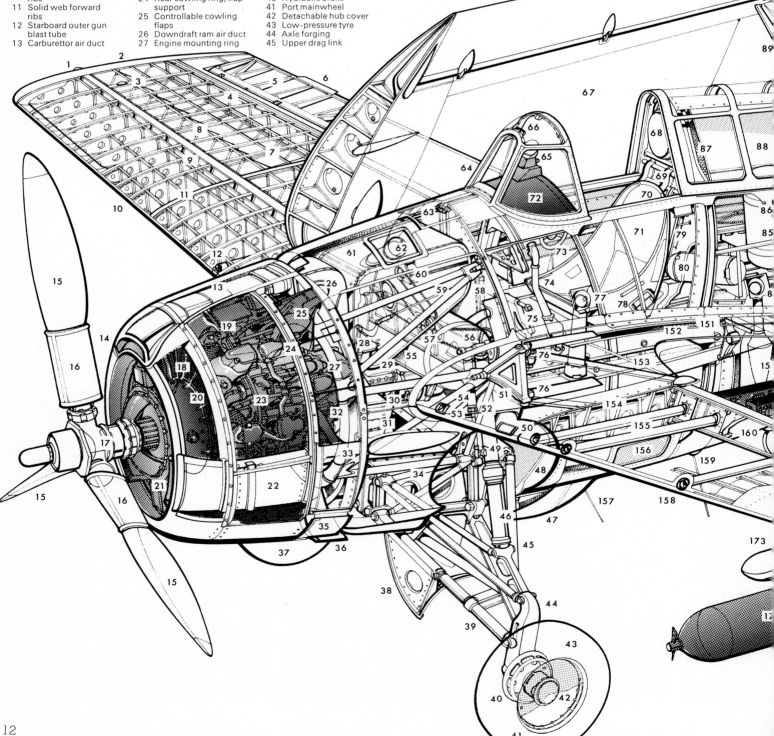

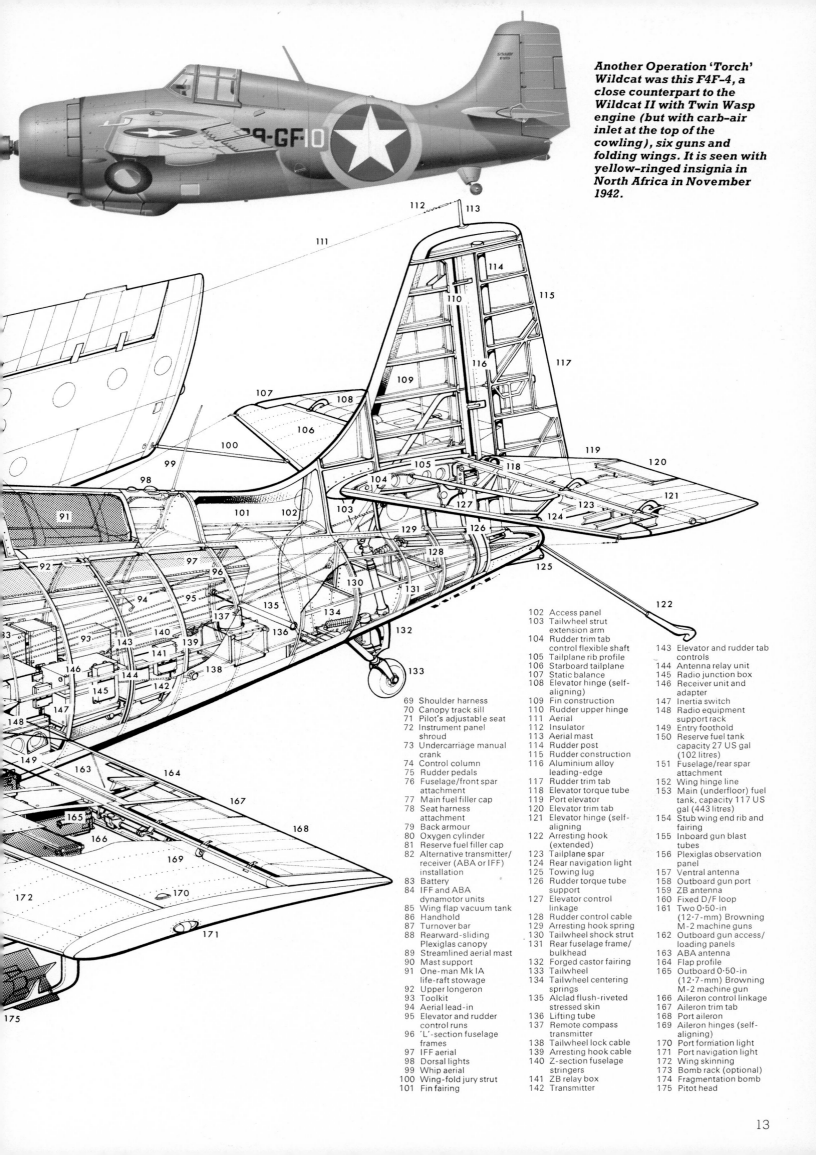

Another Operation 'Torch' Wildcat was this F4F-4, a close counterpart to the Wildcat II with Twin Wasp engine (but with carb-air inlet at the top of the cowling), six guns and folding wings. It is seen with yellow-ringed insignia in North Africa in November 1942.

69 Shoulder harness
70 Canopy track sill
71 Pilot's adjustable seat
72 Instrument panel shroud
73 Undercarriage manual crank
74 Control column
75 Rudder pedals
76 Fuselage/front spar attachment
77 Main fuel filler cap
78 Seat harness attachment
79 Back armour
80 Oxygen cylinder
81 Reserve fuel filler cap
82 Alternative transmitter/receiver (ABA or IFF) installation
83 Battery
84 IFF and ABA dynamotor units
85 Wing flap vacuum tank
86 Handhold
87 Turnover bar
88 Rearward-sliding Plexiglas canopy
89 Streamlined aerial mast
90 Mast support
91 One-man Mk IA life-raft stowage
92 Upper longeron
93 Toolkit
94 Aerial lead-in
95 Elevator and rudder control runs
96 'L'-section fuselage frames
97 IFF aerial
98 Dorsal lights
99 Whip aerial
100 Wing-fold jury strut
101 Fin fairing

102 Access panel
103 Tailwheel strut extension arm
104 Rudder trim tab control flexible shaft
105 Tailplane rib profile
106 Starboard tailplane
107 Static balance
108 Elevator hinge (self-aligning)
109 Fin construction
110 Rudder upper hinge
111 Aerial
112 Insulator
113 Aerial mast
114 Rudder post
115 Rudder construction
116 Aluminium alloy leading-edge
117 Rudder trim tab
118 Elevator torque tube
119 Port elevator
120 Elevator trim tab
121 Elevator hinge (self-aligning
122 Arresting hook (extended)
123 Tailplane spar
124 Rear navigation light
125 Towing lug
126 Rudder torque tube support
127 Elevator control linkage
128 Rudder control cable
129 Arresting hook spring
130 Tailwheel shock strut
131 Rear fuselage frame/bulkhead
132 Forged castor fairing
133 Tailwheel
134 Tailwheel centering springs
135 Alclad flush-riveted stressed skin
136 Lifting tube
137 Remote compass transmitter
138 Tailwheel lock cable
139 Arresting hook cable
140 Z-section fuselage stringers
141 ZB relay box
142 Transmitter

143 Elevator and rudder tab controls
144 Antenna relay unit
145 Radio junction box
146 Receiver unit and adapter
147 Inertia switch
148 Radio equipment support rack
149 Entry foothold
150 Reserve fuel tank capacity 27 US gal (102 litres)
151 Fuselage/rear spar attachment
152 Wing hinge line
153 Main (underfloor) fuel tank, capacity 117 US gal (443 litres)
154 Stub wing end rib and fairing
155 Inboard gun blast tubes
156 Plexiglas observation panel
157 Ventral antenna
158 Outboard gun port
159 ZB antenna
160 Fixed D/F loop
161 Two 0·50-in (12·7-mm) Browning M-2 machine guns
162 Outboard gun access/loading panels
163 ABA antenna
164 Flap profile
165 Outboard 0·50-in (12·7-mm) Browning M-2 machine gun
166 Aileron control linkage
167 Aileron trim tab
168 Port aileron
169 Aileron hinges (self-aligning)
170 Port formation light
171 Port navigation light
172 Wing skinning
173 Bomb rack (optional)
174 Fragmentation bomb
175 Pitot head

The First Round

Well-worn Bell P-39Ds photographed in 1942 at a training unit at Dale Mabry Field near Tallahassee, Florida, with the numbering of the 31st Pursuit Group faintly showing under the large numerals. Designed around the massive 37-mm cannon, the P-39 had good punch but unimpressive performance.

larger engine in the Wildcat so that its performance might be improved.

And so, when war finally came to the United States, the renamed US Army Air Force had on hand a fighter strength composed largely of Curtiss P-40s, with a few Curtiss P-36s and Republic P-35s in overseas locations, and a very few Bell P-39s defending the west coast against a feared enemy air attack. The US Navy and US Marines had the majority of their fighter squadrons equipped with Grumman Wildcats. A single squadron of Brewster F2A-3 aircraft was operating from the USS Lexington, flown by enlisted chief petty officer pilots of Fighting Squadron (VF) 2. The US Marine Corps flew a mix of Wildcats and Brewsters.

With this force of unproven fighters, American pilots lifted off to meet the tough and determined onslaught of highly-skilled, well trained Japanese pilots flying a very superior fighter: the Mitsubishi Type Zero.

Early morning, 7 December 1941, and A6M2 fighters and B5N2 torpedo bombers are about to take off from the Imperial Navy carrier Hiryu. As 'Zeke' and 'Kate' these types were to become familiar to every US serviceman in the Pacific.

American Fighters of World War II

Even the first prototype Lockheed XP–38 had handed (oppositely rotating) propellers, but in almost all other respects it differed from the production P–38. Here the first of these strange birds is parked at March Field on 31 December 1938, after coming by road from Burbank.

Fighter sketches

Seversky (Republic) P-35: designed originally as the Seversky SEV-1XP for a USAAC competition of August 1935, it was re-engined and redesignated P-35. The USAAC ordered 77 on 16 June 1936. P-35s served with 17th, 27th and 94th Pursuit Squadrons (1st Pursuit Group) between 1938 and 1940, sharing flight time with Curtiss P-36 equipment assigned to the same squadrons in a service test competition. The USAAC diverted 48 from a Swedish order for the defence of the Philippines in October 1940. By 7 December 1941, the P-35 equipped only the 34th Pursuit Squadron based near Manila. The little fighters saw combat in the area during December, and two survived to join the 'Bamboo Fleet' on Bataan. Both were lost subsequently to enemy action.

Curtiss P-36: derived from the fixed-gear Hawk 75 of 1934, this trim pursuit lost an initial competition to the P-35, but won the later and more important one of May 1937. The USAAC ordered 210 on 6 June 1937, in the largest US fighter order since World War I. Deliveries began in April 1938, with early assignments to the 1st, 8th, 16th, 18th and 20th Pursuit Groups. Considered obsolescent by December 1941, the P-36 was relegated to the training role in the USA, but some were still on active rosters in the Canal Zone and Hawaii. Several of the latter survived the initial Japanese attack at Pearl Harbor, intercepted a formation of torpedo planes and flamed two.

Apart from the fairings for the main landing gears this might be a production F6F Hellcat. In fact it was the prototype, with designation XF6F–3, flown with the Double Wasp engine on 30 July 1942.

The First Round

The chief attributes of the Brewster F2A-3 (Buffalo) were good manoeuvrability and a comfortable cockpit with all-round vision. Sadly, it was inferior to the Japanese fighters it encountered, and its combat record was disastrous.

Curtiss P-40 Warhawk: re-engined P-36, the P-40 became the standard USAAC pursuit, replacing both the P-35 and the P-36. Rugged airframe and low cost kept it in production as a stop-gap fighter, buying time to tool for more advanced types. It was immortalized by the American Volunteer Group in China and Burma, and was the most important USAAF fighter in the inventory at the start of the war. A total of 13,740 of all variants was built.

Brewster F2A: the US Navy's first monoplane fighter began development 15 November 1935 and flew first in December 1937. Deliveries to the fleet began in July 1939, but early tests aboard the USS *Lexington* showed landing gear weaknesses. As a stripped, test aeroplane its performance matched those of its 1938 contemporaries; but equipped with armour, extra guns and radio to make it combat-ready, it was only mediocre. By 7 December 1941, US Navy F2As were operational only with VF-2, and that unit was disbanded soon after. The US Marines flew them against overwhelming Japanese air strength during the Battle of Midway, 4 June 1942, and lost 13 out of 20 Brewsters in the air combat. Total production was 509 examples.

Grumman F4F Wildcat: originally designed as a biplane in a competition—which it lost—with the Brewster F2A, the Wildcat went on to become the US Navy's first-line fighter at the start of the war. It had been redesigned and re-engined, ordered by the US Navy in September 1938, and delivered to the fleet beginning in late 1940. When the Japanese attacked, the Wildcat was the mainstay of US Navy and US Marine fighting squadrons, equipping 10 out of the established 13. Although easily outmanoeuvred by the lightly loaded Japanese fighters, Wildcats combined heavy armament and rugged construction with pilot skills and tactics to rack up a kill ratio of nearly 7:1. Production totalled 7,344.

A massive fighter, with the biggest propeller then fitted to any fighter, the Vought XF4U-1 first flew on 20 May 1940. Five months later it became the first American fighter to exceed 400 mph (644 km/h), one of the results being termination of Pratt & Whitney's programme for liquid-cooled engines.

The Army Attackers

The USAAF fighters of 1941 had sad failings. But in the pipeline were some classic aircraft that soon gave the service real teeth in the escort and ground-attack missions.

North American P-51 Mustangs over England, 1944. The closest three are P-51Ds with the fourth aircraft a P-51B.

Five American aircraft shouldered the bulk of the fighter combat action for the USAAF during World War II: the Lockheed P-38 Lightning, Bell P-39 Airacobra, Curtiss P-40 Warhawk, Republic P-47 Thunderbolt and North American P-51 Mustang. Additionally, a substantial and often overlooked share of the fighting was done with Supermarine Spitfires, equipping a number of American units through a reverse Lend-Lease arrangement.

Each of these fighters had been under development, and at least one prototype of each had flown and been tested, before war reached the United States in December 1941. Furthermore, production lines—spurred on by enormous support from foreign orders, particularly from the

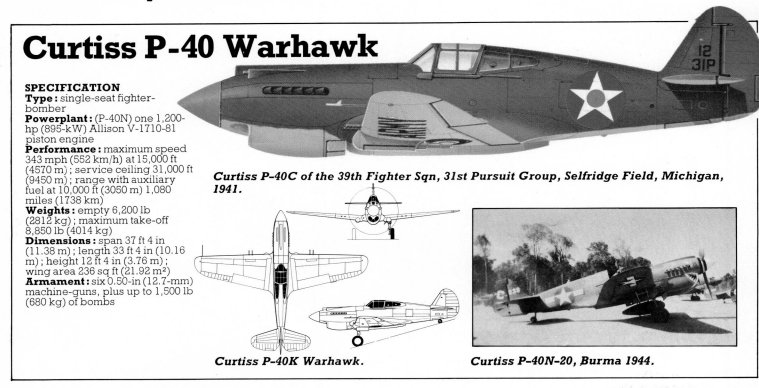

Curtiss P-40 Warhawk

SPECIFICATION
Type: single-seat fighter-bomber
Powerplant: (P-40N) one 1,200-hp (895-kW) Allison V-1710-81 piston engine
Performance: maximum speed 343 mph (552 km/h) at 15,000 ft (4570 m); service ceiling 31,000 ft (9450 m); range with auxiliary fuel at 10,000 ft (3050 m) 1,080 miles (1738 km)
Weights: empty 6,200 lb (2812 kg); maximum take-off 8,850 lb (4014 kg)
Dimensions: span 37 ft 4 in (11.38 m); length 33 ft 4 in (10.16 m); height 12 ft 4 in (3.76 m); wing area 236 sq ft (21.92 m²)
Armament: six 0.50-in (12.7-mm) machine-guns, plus up to 1,500 lb (680 kg) of bombs

Curtiss P-40C of the 39th Fighter Sqn, 31st Pursuit Group, Selfridge Field, Michigan, 1941.

Curtiss P-40K Warhawk.

Curtiss P-40N-20, Burma 1944.

British and French —were beginning to turn out quantities of fighters, as well as other types. American fighters were, at that stage of their development, almost universally unfitted for contemporary combat: their armament was light; the use of armour was minimal; self-sealing tanks were still being developed; and radio equipment was very basic. The fighter force of the United States was then, as it has too often been, best suited for daytime, good-weather fighting against inferior numbers.

In retrospect, one wonders just what tactical thinking was behind the specifications often issued by the USAAC for its fighters. They seem to have been written for some unimagined contest, where the enemy flew straight and level in bright sunshine at no higher than 10,000 ft

Six of the first Republic P-47B Thunderbolts to be delivered to a fighting unit, the 56th Fighter Group, USAAF. This unit transferred to England in 1943 and eventually notched up the highest air combat score (674½) in all US forces during World War II.

A P-47D-25-RE (Farmingdale) serving with one of the fighter squadrons of the 8th Air Force in England: the 352nd Fighter Sqn of the 353rd Fighter Group, based at Raydon, Suffolk.

A colourful P-47D-30-RA, with dorsal fin, serving with the occupation forces in Germany in the summer of 1945. The unit was the 512th Fighter Sqn of the 406th Fighter Group.

One of the last of the 'razorback' variety, this Evansville-built P-47D was assigned to the Pacific theatre and is pictured serving with the 19th Fighter Sqn, 318th Fighter Group, based on Saipan island in the summer of 1944. Though generally adequate, the original canopy produced a 20° blind spot at the rear.

(3050 m) and no faster than 200 mph (320 km/h). Moreover, enemy aircraft apparently were assumed to be incapable of defending themselves. The reality of air combat never intruded into the paragraphs of the pre-war specifications that defined the shape and performance of an entire generation of American combat planes.

Freelance operations

As a result, Americans got the worst of it in the early air fighting. There was, happily for national morale at the time, one exception: the American Volunteer Group. That organization, brilliantly led by Claire Chennault, a fighter tactician retired from the USAAC, racked up an astonishing victory string against first-ranked Japanese pilots in China and Burma. They used Chennault's basic concepts for effective defensive fighter operations: first, detect and report the

Republic P-47 Thunderbolt

SPECIFICATION
Type: single-seat escort fighter and fighter-bomber
Powerplant: (P-47N) one 2,800-hp (2088-kW) Pratt & Whitney R-2800-77 radial piston engine
Performance: maximum speed 467 mph (752 km/h) at 32,500 ft (9905 m); cruising speed 300 mph (483 km/h); service ceiling 43,000 ft (13105 m); range on internal fuel 800 miles (1287 km)
Weights: empty 11,000 lb (4990 kg); maximum take-off 20,700 lb (9389 kg)
Dimensions: span 42 ft 7 in (12.28 m); length 36 ft 1 in (11.0 m); height 14 ft 7 in (4.44 m); wing area 322 sq ft (29.91 m²)
Armament: six or eight 0.50-in (12.7-mm) machine-guns, plus up to 2,000 lb (907 kg) of bombs or ten 5-in (127-mm) rocket projectiles

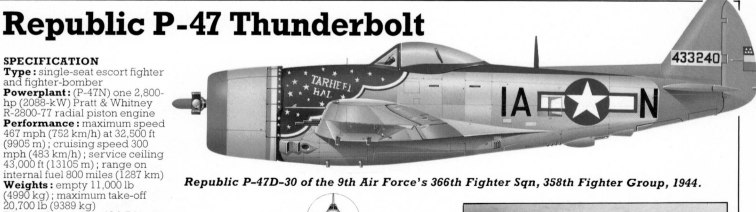

Republic P-47D-30 of the 9th Air Force's 366th Fighter Sqn, 358th Fighter Group, 1944.

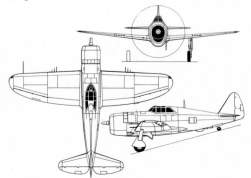

Republic P-47C Thunderbolt

Thunderbolts (P-47Ds and P-47C) of the 78th Fighter Group, England, 1944.

The Army Attackers

Republic P-47D-10 Thunderbolt cutaway drawing key

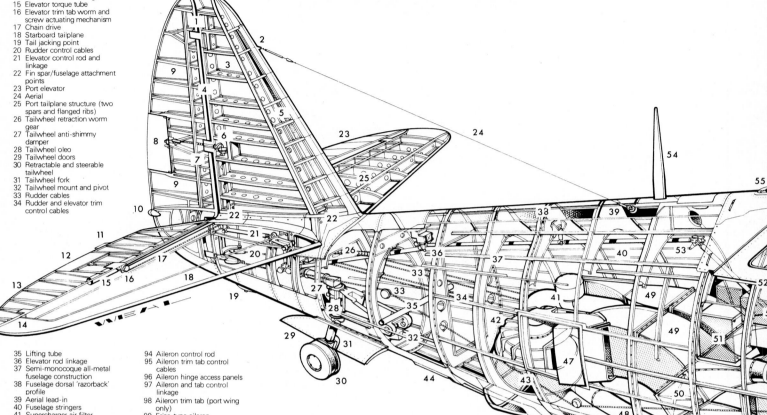

1 Rudder upper hinge
2 Aerial attachment
3 Fin flanged ribs
4 Rudder post/fin aft spar
5 Fin front spar
6 Rudder trim tab worm and screw actuating mechanism (chain driven)
7 Rudder centre hinge
8 Rudder trim tab
9 Rudder structure
10 Tail navigation light
11 Elevator fixed tab
12 Elevator trim tab
13 Starboard elevator structure
14 Elevator outboard hinge
15 Elevator torque tube
16 Elevator trim tab worm and screw actuating mechanism
17 Chain drive
18 Starboard tailplane
19 Tail jacking point
20 Rudder control cables
21 Elevator control rod and linkage
22 Fin spar/fuselage attachment points
23 Port elevator
24 Aerial
25 Port tailplane structure (two spars and flanged ribs)
26 Tailwheel retraction worm gear
27 Tailwheel anti-shimmy damper
28 Tailwheel oleo
29 Tailwheel doors
30 Retractable and steerable tailwheel
31 Tailwheel fork
32 Tailwheel mount and pivot
33 Rudder cables
34 Rudder and elevator trim control cables

35 Lifting tube
36 Elevator rod linkage
37 Semi-monocoque all-metal fuselage construction
38 Fuselage dorsal 'razorback' profile
39 Aerial lead-in
40 Fuselage stringers
41 Supercharger air filter
42 Supercharger
43 Turbine casing
44 Turbosupercharger compartment air vent
45 Turbosupercharger exhaust hood fairing (stainless steel)
46 Outlet louvres
47 Intercooler exhaust doors (port and starboard)
48 Exhaust pipes
49 Cooling air ducts
50 Intercooler unit (cooling and supercharged air)
51 Radio transmitter and receiver packs (Detrola)
52 Canopy track
53 Elevator rod linkage
54 Aerial mast
55 Formation light
56 Rearward-vision frame cut-out and glazing
57 Oxygen bottles
58 Supercharged and cooling air pipe (supercharger to carburettor) port
59 Elevator linkage
60 Supercharged and cooling air pipe (supercharger to carburettor) starboard
61 Central duct (to intercooler unit)
62 Wingroot air louvres
63 Wingroot fillet
64 Auxiliary fuel tank (100 US gal/379 litres)
65 Auxiliary fuel filler point
66 Rudder cable turnbuckle
67 Cockpit floor support
68 Seat adjustment lever
69 Pilot's seat
70 Canopy emergency release (port and starboard)
71 Trim tab controls
72 Back and head armour
73 Headrest
74 Rearward-sliding canopy
75 Rear-view mirror fairing
76 'Vee' windshields with central pillar
77 Internal bulletproof glass screen
78 Gunsight
79 Engine control quadrant (cockpit port wall)
80 Control column
81 Rudder pedals
82 Oxygen regulator
83 Underfloor elevator control quadrant
84 Rudder cable linkage

85 Wing rear spar/fuselage attachment (tapered bolts/bushings)
86 Wing supporting lower bulkhead section
87 Main fuel tank (205 US gal/776 litres)
88 Fuselage forward structure
89 Stainless steel/Alclad firewall bulkhead
90 Cowl flap valve
91 Main fuel filler point
92 Anti-freeze fluid tank
93 Hydraulic reservoir
94 Aileron control rod
95 Aileron trim tab control cables
96 Aileron hinge access panels
97 Aileron and tab control linkage
98 Aileron trim tab (port wing only)
99 Frise-type aileron
100 Wing rear (No. 2) spar
101 Port navigation light
102 Pitot head
103 Wing front (No. 1) spar
104 Wing stressed skin
105 Four-gun ammunition troughs (individual bays)
106 Staggered gun barrels
107 Removable panel
108 Inter-spar gun bay access panel
109 Forward gunsight bead
110 Oil feed pipes
111 Oil tank (28.6 US gal/108 litres)
112 Hydraulic pressure line
113 Engine upper bearers
114 Engine control correlating cam
115 Eclipse pump (anti-icing)
116 Fuel level transmitter
117 Generator
118 Battery junction box
119 Storage battery
120 Exhaust collector ring
121 Cowl flap actuating cylinder
122 Exhaust outlets to collector ring
123 Cowl flaps
124 Supercharged and cooling air ducts to carburettor (port and starboard)
125 Exhaust upper outlets
126 Cowling frame
127 Pratt & Whitney R-2800-59 18-cylinder twin-row engine
128 Cowling nose panel
129 Magnetos
130 Propeller governor
131 Propeller hub
132 Reduction gear casing
133 Spinner
134 Propeller cuffs
135 Four-blade Curtiss constant-speed electric propeller
136 Oil cooler intakes (port and starboard)
137 Supercharger intercooler (central) air intake
138 Ducting
139 Oil cooler feed pipes
140 Starboard oil cooler
141 Engine lower bearers
142 Oil cooler exhaust variable shutter
143 Fixed deflector
144 Excess exhaust gas gate
145 Belly stores/weapons shackles

146 Metal auxiliary drop tank (75 US gal/284 litres)
147 Inboard mainwheel well door
148 Mainwheel well door actuating cylinder
149 Camera gun port
150 Cabin air-conditioning intake (starboard wing only)
151 Wingroot fairing
152 Wing front spar/fuselage attachment (tapered bolts/bushings)
153 Wing inboard rib mainwheel well recess

154 Wing front (No. 1) spar
155 Undercarriage pivot point
156 Hydraulic retraction cylinder
157 Auxiliary (undercarriage mounting) wing spar
158 Gun bay warm air flexible duct
159 Wing rear (No. 2) spar
160 Landing flap inboard hinge
161 Auxiliary (No. 3) wing spar inboard section (flap mounting)
162 NACA slotted trailing-edge landing flaps
163 Landing flap centre hinge
164 Landing flap hydraulic cylinder
165 Four 0.5-in (12.7-mm) Browning machine guns
166 Inter-spar gun bay inboard rib
167 Ammunition feed chutes
168 Individual ammunition troughs
169 Underwing stores/weapons pylon
170 Landing flap outboard hinge
171 Flap door
172 Landing flap profile
173 Aileron fixed tab (starboard wing only)
174 Frise-type aileron structure
175 Aileron hinge/steel forging spar attachments
176 Auxiliary (No. 3) wing spar outboard section (aileron mounting)
177 Multi-cellular wing construction
178 Wing outboard ribs
179 Wingtip structure
180 Starboard navigation light
181 Leading-edge rib sections
182 Bomb shackles
183 500-lb (227-kg) M43 demolition bomb
184 Undercarriage leg fairing (overlapping upper section)
185 Mainwheel fairing (lower section)
186 Wheel fork
187 Starboard mainwheel
188 Brake lines
189 Landing gear air-oil shock strut
190 Machine gun barrel blast tubes
191 Staggered gun barrels
192 Rocket-launcher slide bar
193 Centre strap
194 Front mount (attached below front spar between inboard pair of guns)
195 Deflector arms
196 Triple-tube 4.5-in (11.5-cm) rocket-launcher (Type M10)
197 Front retaining band
198 4.5-in (11.5-cm) M8 rocket projectile

PILOT PRESS
COPYRIGHT
DRAWING

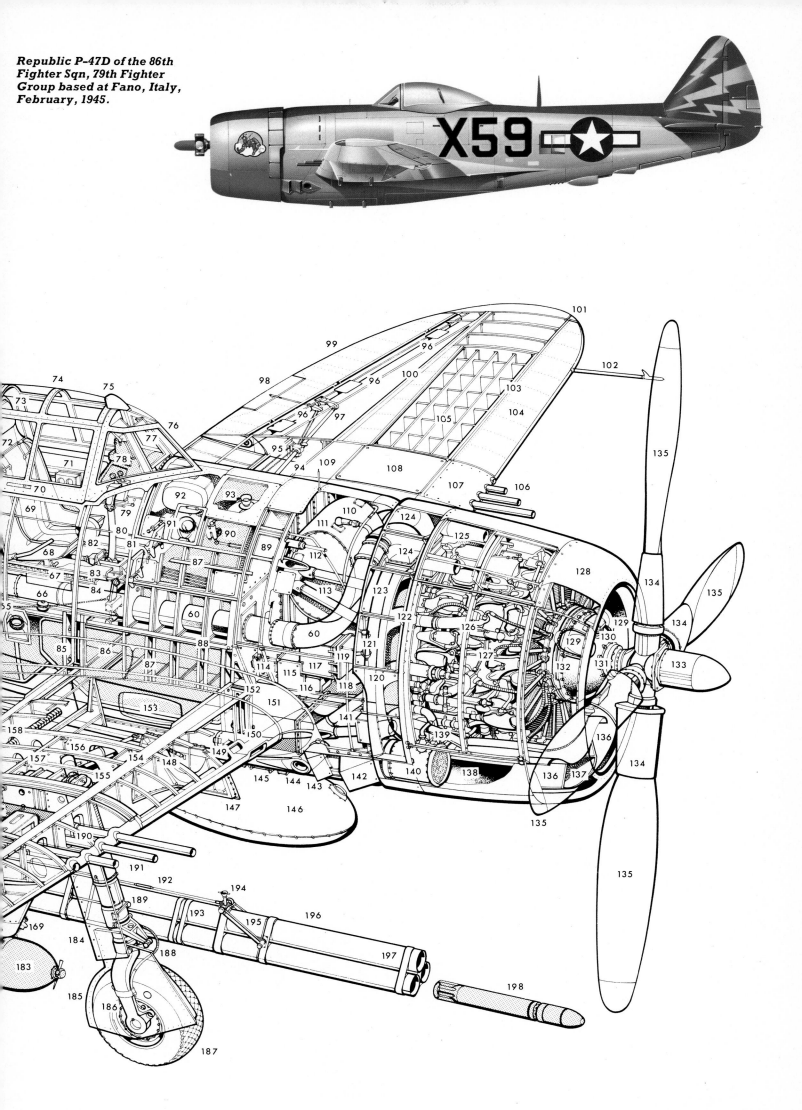

Republic P-47D of the 86th Fighter Sqn, 79th Fighter Group based at Fano, Italy, February, 1945.

X59

Republic P-47 Thunderbolt

Fighter-bomber par excellence, the P-47D is seen here with bombs of the 1,000-lb (454-kg) size hung under the wing pylons and one of the nine types of drop tank and napalm carried on the centreline. This particular aircraft, a P-47D-25-RE, served with the 527th Fighter Sqn of the 86th Fighter Group. This was one of the leading fighter groups in the Medittanean theatre; it fought its way from North Africa through Sicily into Italy, and equipped with P-47Ds in 1944. It then operated intensively not only in ground attack on Kesselring's retreating forces in Italy but also over the Balkans and on long-range escort duties of B-24s (occasionally other bombers) as far as Berlin. The principal home base for 'Rabbit' was Pisa. Note that the stripes of the 86th Fighter Group have obliterated the USAAF tail number.

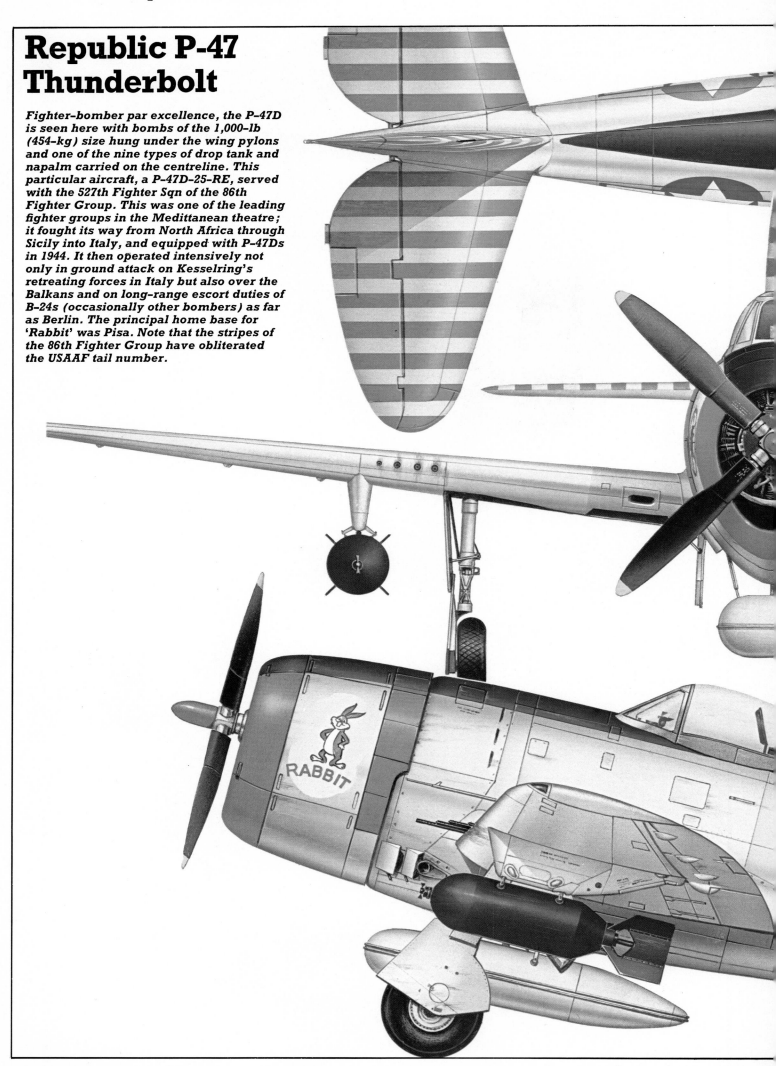

Wearing the short-lived (July/September 1943) red-bordered insignia, the F-5B was the final form of unarmed photo-reconnaissance Lightning. A P-38J fighter, in regular olive-drab finish, keeps company.

Bell P-39 Airacobra

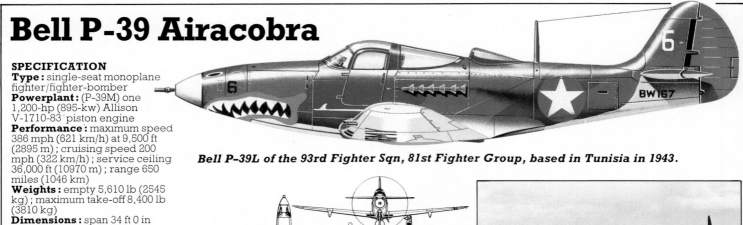

SPECIFICATION
Type: single-seat monoplane fighter/fighter-bomber
Powerplant: (P-39M) one 1,200-hp (895-kw) Allison V-1710-83 piston engine
Performance: maximum speed 386 mph (621 km/h) at 9,500 ft (2895 m); cruising speed 200 mph (322 km/h); service ceiling 36,000 ft (10970 m); range 650 miles (1046 km)
Weights: empty 5,610 lb (2545 kg); maximum take-off 8,400 lb (3810 kg)
Dimensions: span 34 ft 0 in (10.36 m); length 30 ft 2 in (9.19 m); height 11 ft 10 in (3.61 m); wing area 213 sq ft (19.79 m²)
Armament: one 37-mm T9 cannon, two 0.50-in (12.7-mm) machine-guns and four 0.30-in (7.62-mm) machine-guns, plus provision for one 500-lb (227-kg) bomb

Bell P-39L of the 93rd Fighter Sqn, 81st Fighter Group, based in Tunisia in 1943.

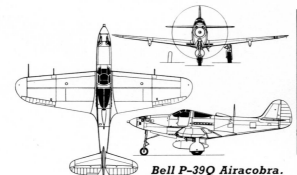

Bell P-39Q Airacobra.

target; second, intercept it; third, shoot it down. The AVG's early model P-40s, universally regarded as mediocre fighters by everybody else, became terrible weapons in the hands of skilled and daring pilots who turned the faults of the plane into virtues.

A tough education

Tactics and the proper use of fighters made the AVG effective, though outnumbered, and that lesson had to be learned over and over again by young pilots coming into combat for the first time. Those who learned, survived.

As one result of improperly written requirements, and the evolution of tactics, specific fighters designed to do one task often found their best employment in another. Republic's P-47 Thunderbolt was one example. Designed as a high-altitude fighter, it first became a bomber escort, and then a superb ground-support aircraft, able to haul enormous loads of ordnance and deliver bombs on target. The Lockheed P-38 Lightning was another. Designed as an interceptor, it lacked the manoeuvrability for one-on-one combat against its principal adversary in the Pacific. But it was used as a superlative long-range fighter-bomber in that theatre and in Europe, where it also served effectively as an escort to the bomber fleets.

As the war situation changed, so did the general role of fighters. One early mission was escorting and protecting bombers. The pre-war USAAC had blundered badly in not appreciat-

Lockheed P-38 Lightning

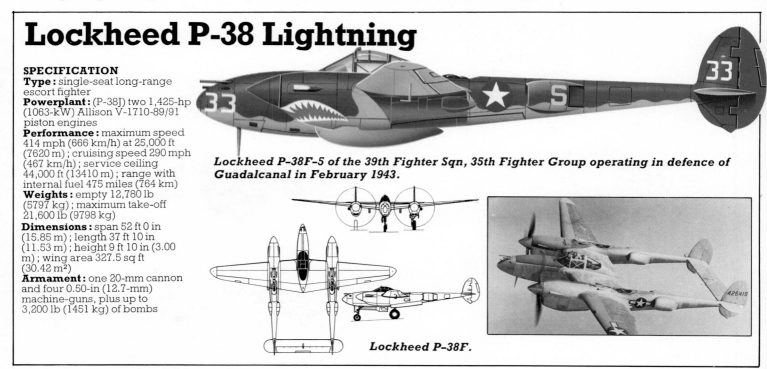

SPECIFICATION
Type: single-seat long-range escort fighter
Powerplant: (P-38J) two 1,425-hp (1063-kW) Allison V-1710-89/91 piston engines
Performance: maximum speed 414 mph (666 km/h) at 25,000 ft (7620 m); cruising speed 290 mph (467 km/h); service ceiling 44,000 ft (13410 m); range with internal fuel 475 miles (764 km)
Weights: empty 12,780 lb (5797 kg); maximum take-off 21,600 lb (9798 kg)
Dimensions: span 52 ft 0 in (15.85 m); length 37 ft 10 in (11.53 m); height 9 ft 10 in (3.00 m); wing area 327.5 sq ft (30.42 m²)
Armament: one 20-mm cannon and four 0.50-in (12.7-mm) machine-guns, plus up to 3,200 lb (1451 kg) of bombs

Lockheed P-38F-5 of the 39th Fighter Sqn, 35th Fighter Group operating in defence of Guadalcanal in February 1943.

Lockheed P-38F.

Above : This P–38H was one of the last of the Lightning family to come off the Burbank line with the old engine installation with only flush oil–cooler inlets under the engine and intercooler radiators in the leading edge. Deep chin radiators followed on the P–38J.

ing the need for special escort fighters for the heavyweights. Pressed into service, although incapable of performing the mission effectively, the fighters and their pilots received undeserved criticism every time a bomber was lost. But the fighters at that time were range-limited, and could not go with the bombers to the targets deep in Germany. Drop tanks, hurriedly developed and employed, were some help; but the truly effective use of escorts had to await the long-range Mustang.

Hammering the enemy

Increasingly, fighters were turned toward ground support as a major mission. They became, in effect, a winged heavy artillery, an added supporting strength that enabled ground forces to move more rapidly and securely. With an air umbrella above, and other aircraft down 'in the mud' with the infantry, air power made major contributions to all the ground battles.

As the war moved to its inevitable conclusion, both German and Japanese air strength waned rapidly. With little opposition in the skies of Europe, American fighters ranged across the continent, bombing and strafing ground targets on interdiction missions, or hammering a German armoured column in support; taught the subtleties of long-range cruise control by visiting veteran pilot Charles Lindbergh, they also smashed Japanese air power on the ground at one Pacific island base after another.

Lockheed P–38K Lightning of the 338th Fighter Sqn, 55th Fighter Group, 8th Air Force, based at Nuthampstead, spring 1944.

Lockheed P–38J Lightning of the 401st Fighter Sqn, 370th Fighter Group, based at Florennes, Belgium, in November 1944.

27

Lockheed P-38 Lightning

'Jeanne' was a P–38J–15–LO, serial number 43–28430, assembled at Lockheed's plant in Burbank, California, and sent to join the 55th Fighter Sqn of the 8th Air Force's 20th Fighter Group. She was based at Kingscliffe, Northants, in Great Britain, and at one time her placarded nose recorded one enemy aircraft destroyed, along with two locomotives and a torpedo boat, plus participation in nine fighter sweeps, two bombing raids, and 30 escort missions.

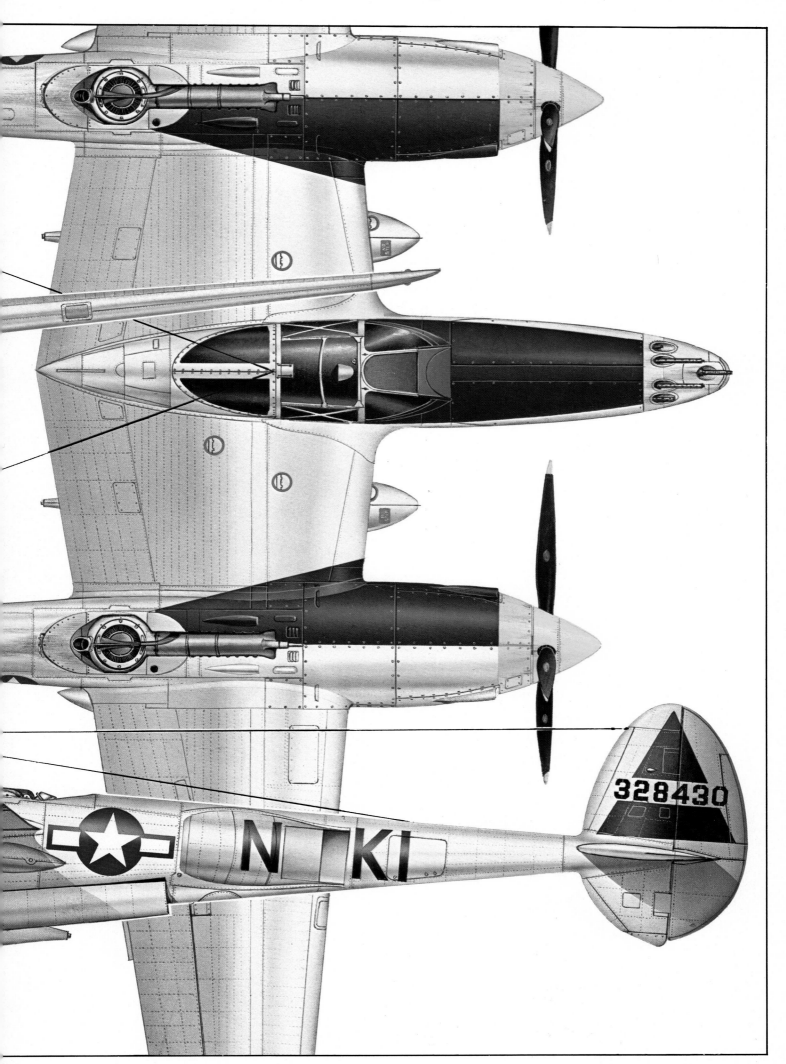

328430

N KI

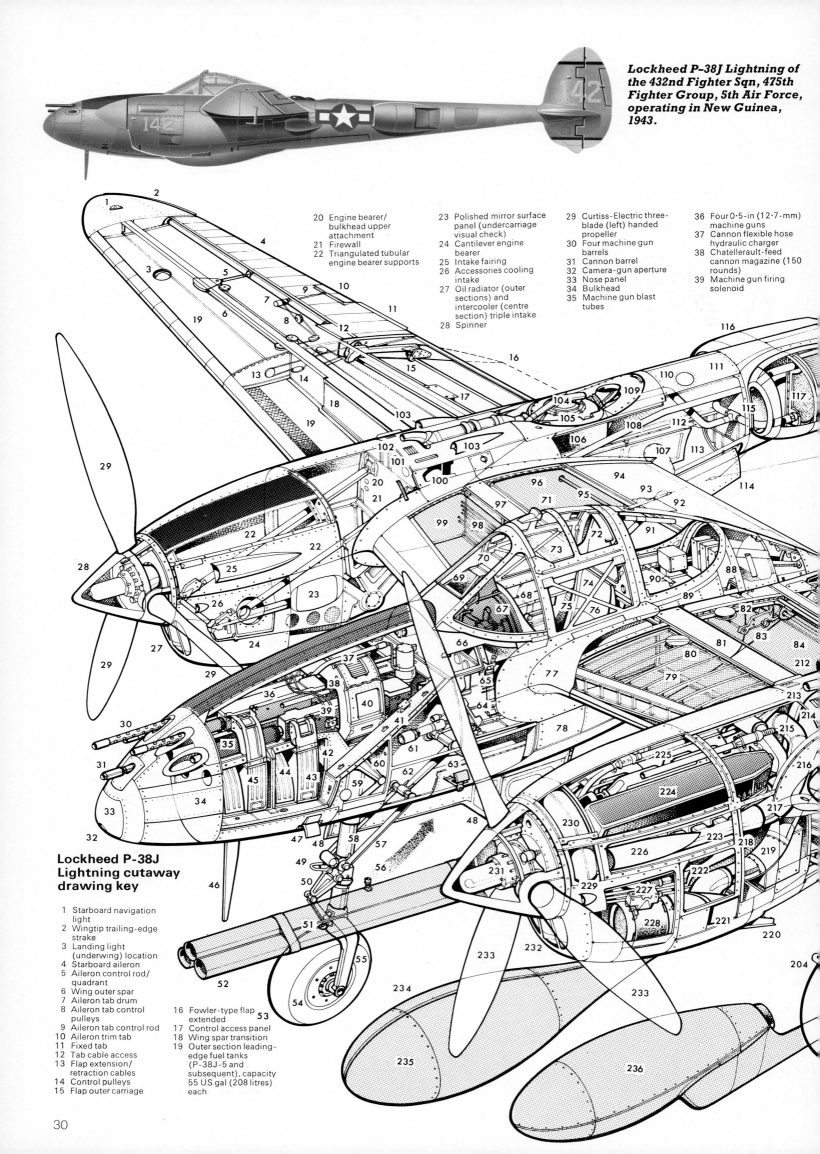

Lockheed P-38J Lightning of the 432nd Fighter Sqn, 475th Fighter Group, 5th Air Force, operating in New Guinea, 1943.

20 Engine bearer/ bulkhead upper attachment
21 Firewall
22 Triangulated tubular engine bearer supports
23 Polished mirror surface panel (undercarriage visual check)
24 Cantilever engine bearer
25 Intake fairing
26 Accessories cooling intake
27 Oil radiator (outer sections) and intercooler (centre section) triple intake
28 Spinner
29 Curtiss-Electric three-blade (left) handed propeller
30 Four machine gun barrels
31 Cannon barrel
32 Camera-gun aperture
33 Nose panel
34 Bulkhead
35 Machine gun blast tubes
36 Four 0·5-in (12·7-mm) machine guns
37 Cannon flexible hose hydraulic charger
38 Chatellerault-feed cannon magazine (150 rounds)
39 Machine gun firing solenoid

Lockheed P-38J Lightning cutaway drawing key

1 Starboard navigation light
2 Wingtip trailing-edge strake
3 Landing light (underwing) location
4 Starboard aileron
5 Aileron control rod/ quadrant
6 Wing outer spar
7 Aileron tab drum
8 Aileron tab control pulleys
9 Aileron tab control rod
10 Aileron trim tab
11 Fixed tab
12 Tab cable access
13 Flap extension/ retraction cables
14 Control pulleys
15 Flap outer carriage
16 Fowler-type flap extended
17 Control access panel
18 Wing spar transition
19 Outer section leading-edge fuel tanks (P-38J-5 and subsequent), capacity 55 US gal (208 litres) each

30

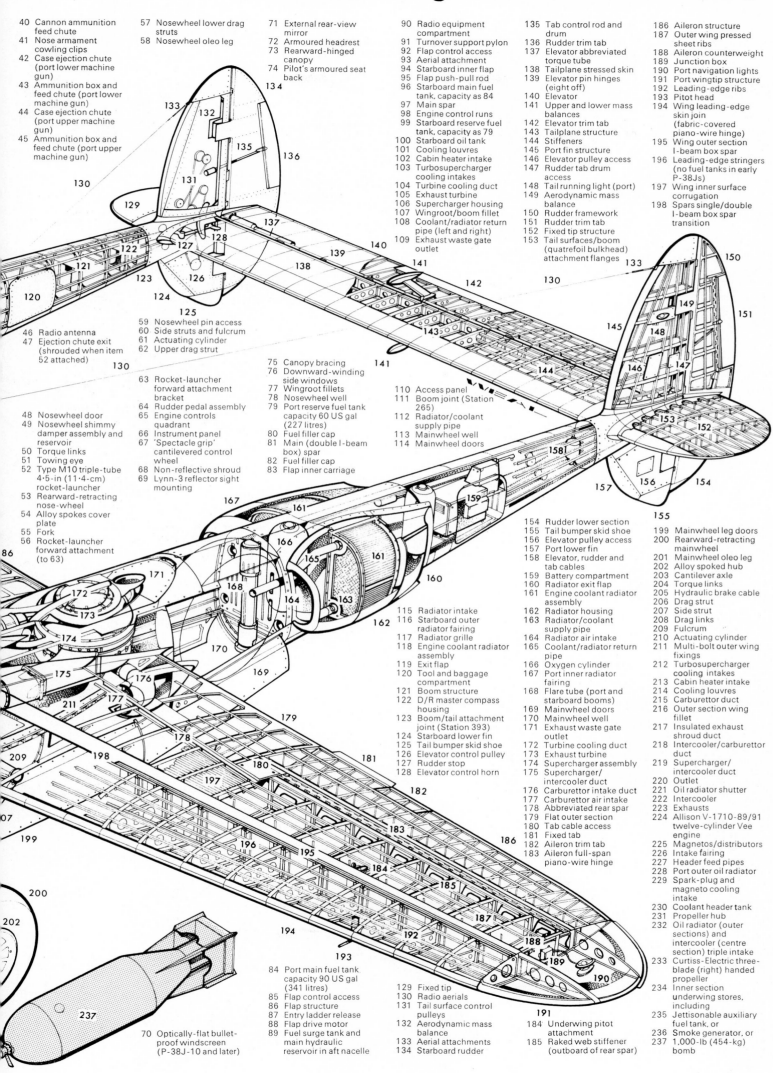

40 Cannon ammunition feed chute
41 Nose armament cowling clips
42 Case ejection chute (port lower machine gun)
43 Ammunition box and feed chute (port lower machine gun)
44 Case ejection chute (port upper machine gun)
45 Ammunition box and feed chute (port upper machine gun)

46 Radio antenna
47 Ejection chute exit (shrouded when item 52 attached)

48 Nosewheel door
49 Nosewheel shimmy damper assembly and reservoir
50 Torque links
51 Towing eye
52 Type M10 triple-tube 4·5-in (11·4-cm) rocket-launcher
53 Rearward-retracting nose-wheel
54 Alloy spokes cover plate
55 Fork
56 Rocket-launcher forward attachment (to 63)

57 Nosewheel lower drag struts
58 Nosewheel oleo leg

59 Nosewheel pin access
60 Side struts and fulcrum
61 Actuating cylinder
62 Upper drag strut

63 Rocket-launcher forward attachment bracket
64 Rudder pedal assembly
65 Engine controls quadrant
66 Instrument panel
67 'Spectacle grip' cantilevered control wheel
68 Non-reflective shroud
69 Lynn-3 reflector sight mounting

70 Optically-flat bullet-proof windscreen (P-38J-10 and later)

71 External rear-view mirror
72 Armoured headrest
73 Rearward-hinged canopy
74 Pilot's armoured seat back

75 Canopy bracing
76 Downward-winding side windows
77 Wingroot fillets
78 Nosewheel well
79 Port reserve fuel tank capacity 60 US gal (227 litres)
80 Fuel filler cap
81 Main (double I-beam box) spar
82 Fuel filler cap
83 Flap inner carriage

84 Port main fuel tank capacity 90 US gal (341 litres)
85 Flap control access
86 Flap structure
87 Entry ladder release
88 Flap drive motor
89 Fuel surge tank and main hydraulic reservoir in aft nacelle

90 Radio equipment compartment
91 Turnover support pylon
92 Flap control access
93 Aerial attachment
94 Starboard inner flap
95 Flap push-pull rod
96 Starboard main fuel tank, capacity as 84
97 Main spar
98 Engine control runs
99 Starboard reserve fuel tank, capacity as 79
100 Starboard oil tank
101 Cooling louvres
102 Cabin heater intake
103 Turbosupercharger cooling intakes
104 Turbine cooling duct
105 Exhaust turbine
106 Supercharger housing
107 Wingroot/boom fillet
108 Coolant/radiator return pipe (left and right)
109 Exhaust waste gate outlet

110 Access panel
111 Boom joint (Station 265)
112 Radiator/coolant supply pipe
113 Mainwheel well
114 Mainwheel doors

115 Radiator intake
116 Starboard outer radiator fairing
117 Radiator grille
118 Engine coolant radiator assembly
119 Exit flap
120 Tool and baggage compartment
121 Boom structure
122 D/R master compass housing
123 Boom/tail attachment joint (Station 393)
124 Starboard lower fin
125 Tail bumper skid shoe
126 Elevator control pulley
127 Rudder stop
128 Elevator control horn

129 Fixed tip
130 Radio aerials
131 Tail surface control pulleys
132 Aerodynamic mass balance
133 Aerial attachments
134 Starboard rudder

135 Tab control rod and drum
136 Rudder trim tab
137 Elevator abbreviated torque tube
138 Tailplane stressed skin
139 Elevator pin hinges (eight off)
140 Elevator
141 Upper and lower mass balances
142 Elevator trim tab
143 Tailplane structure
144 Stiffeners
145 Port fin structure
146 Elevator pulley access
147 Rudder tab drum access
148 Tail running light (port)
149 Aerodynamic mass balance
150 Rudder framework
151 Rudder trim tab
152 Fixed tip structure
153 Tail surfaces/boom (quatrefoil bulkhead) attachment flanges

154 Rudder lower section
155 Tail bumper skid shoe
156 Elevator pulley access
157 Port lower fin
158 Elevator, rudder and tab cables
159 Battery compartment
160 Radiator exit flap
161 Engine coolant radiator assembly
162 Radiator housing
163 Radiator/coolant supply pipe
164 Radiator air intake
165 Coolant/radiator return pipe
166 Oxygen cylinder
167 Port inner radiator fairing
168 Flare tube (port and starboard booms)
169 Mainwheel doors
170 Mainwheel well
171 Exhaust waste gate outlet
172 Turbine cooling duct
173 Exhaust turbine
174 Supercharger assembly
175 Supercharger/intercooler duct
176 Carburettor intake duct
177 Carburettor air intake
178 Abbreviated rear spar
179 Flat outer section
180 Tab cable access
181 Fixed tab
182 Aileron trim tab
183 Aileron full-span piano-wire hinge

184 Underwing pitot attachment
185 Raked web stiffener (outboard of rear spar)

186 Aileron structure
187 Outer wing pressed sheet ribs
188 Aileron counterweight
189 Junction box
190 Port navigation lights
191 Port wingtip structure
192 Leading-edge ribs
193 Pitot head
194 Wing leading-edge skin join (fabric-covered piano-wire hinge)
195 Wing outer section I-beam box spar
196 Leading-edge stringers (no fuel tanks in early P-38Js)
197 Wing inner surface corrugation
198 Spars single/double I-beam box spar transition

199 Mainwheel leg doors
200 Rearward-retracting mainwheel
201 Mainwheel oleo leg
202 Alloy spoked hub
203 Cantilever axle
204 Torque links
205 Hydraulic brake cable
206 Drag strut
207 Side strut
208 Drag links
209 Fulcrum
210 Actuating cylinder
211 Multi-bolt outer wing fixings
212 Turbosupercharger cooling intakes
213 Cabin heater intake
214 Cooling louvres
215 Carburettor duct
216 Outer section wing fillet
217 Insulated exhaust shroud duct
218 Intercooler/carburettor duct
219 Supercharger/intercooler duct
220 Outlet
221 Oil radiator shutter
222 Intercooler
223 Exhausts
224 Allison V-1710-89/91 twelve-cylinder Vee engine
225 Magnetos/distributors
226 Intake fairing
227 Header feed pipes
228 Port outer oil radiator
229 Spark-plug and magneto cooling intake
230 Coolant header tank
231 Propeller hub
232 Oil radiator (outer sections) and intercooler (centre section) triple intake
233 Curtiss-Electric three-blade (right) handed propeller
234 Inner section underwing stores, including
235 Jettisonable auxiliary fuel tank, or
236 Smoke generator, or
237 1,000-lb (454-kg) bomb

North American P-51 Mustang

SPECIFICATION
Type: single-seat interceptor or long-range escort fighter
Powerplant: (P-51D) one 1,695-hp (1264-kW) Packard Merlin V-1650-7 inline piston engine
Performance: maximum speed 437 mph (703 km/h) at 25,000 ft 7620 m); service ceiling 41,900 ft (12770 m); maximum range 2,080 miles (3347 km)
Weights: empty 7,125 lb (3232 kg); maximum take-off 12,100 lb (5488 kg)
Dimensions: span 37 ft 0¼ in (11.28 m); length 32 ft 3 in (9.83 m); height 8 ft 8 in (2.64 m); wing area 233 sq ft (21.65 m²)
Armament: six 0.50-in (12.7-mm) machine-guns, plus up to two 1,000-lb (454-kg) bombs or six 5-in (127-mm) rocket projectiles

North American P-51B Mustang of the 318th Fighter Sqn, 325th Fighter Group, 15th Air Force on the Italian front, 1944.

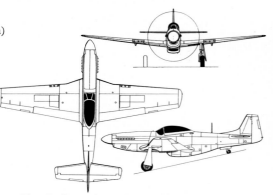

North American P-51D Mustang.

P-51B of 334th FS, 4th FG.

Fighter sketches

Lockheed P-38 Lightning: this was a daring departure from the state of the design art in 1936, when the programme began. The prototype first flew 27 January 1939, and was written off hardly two weeks later following a grandstanding transcontinental speed run. First production quantities were for the British, but without turbosuperchargers and with inevitable weight increases, performance was poor. Deliveries to the USAAF began in June 1941, and by the following April, about 350 were in service but under flight restrictions. Manoeuvrability was sluggish, especially in rolls, so that a P-38 was slow to switch from one manoeuvre to another, and slow to break off combat. Best combat tactics were to bounce the enemy from above at high speed, make one pass through the formation, and climb out. Their final kill ratio in the Pacific was 12:1. By 1944, P-38s cost $134,284 each in production, and the USAAF accepted 9,395 of the type.

Probably repairable, Danny Boy 2 sits on the frost-covered grass of Raydon on 29 December 1944 after bellying in after a combat mission. The P-51D wears the markings of the 350th FS, 353rd FG.

Outward bound to meet the enemy, this P-51D was the mount of Captain John J. Voll, top-scoring US pilot in the Mediterranean theatre with 21 confirmed. He was flying from Mondolfo with the 380th FS, 31st FG (confusingly, letters HL were also used by a P-51D squadron in the British-based 78th FC).

Bell P-39 Airacobra: another radical design, the P-39 featured an engine in the fuselage behind the pilot. Also designed as an interceptor, it was destined to be developed without turbosupercharging and, as a result, it never achieved good high-altitude performance. It was reported to be a dream to fly, with near-perfect control harmony. 'Think the turn,' said one pilot, 'and around she goes.' It had a low service ceiling, a low rate of climb, and a relative lack of manoeuvrability. But it had a rugged airframe. Properly flown, it became an important ground-support aircraft, with the firepower to inflict high damage, and the capacity to absorb punishment. It failed miserably in its first European deployment, and was quickly replaced there; but in the Pacific, it served well and faithfully as a bomber escort, interceptor of Japanese air raids, and as an attacker against ground targets. The US Army accepted 9,558 of them, although most of them were sent to the Russians. USAAF peak inventory was 2,150. By 1944, their cost was down to about $50,000 per plane.

The P-51A was the original USAAF version, with only four 0.5-in (12.7-mm) guns (all in the wings) and provision for bombs or other stores under the wings. This example, with a direction-finding loop antenna on the rear fuselage, was flown by the 1st Air Commando's CO, Colonel Philip Cochran, in Burma in 1944.

Original USAAF production variant of North American P-51 with four 20-mm cannon with the 154th Fighter Sqn in Tunisia and Sicily in 1943.

The Army Attackers

Curtiss P-40 Warhawk: begun as a basically simple re-engining of the tenth P-36, the P-40 gained a combat record that won it final and grudging respect from its detractors. It was the standard pursuit plane when the USA entered the war, and had already been in combat with the Flying Tigers in China. It entered combat with the USAAF on 7 December 1941, and stayed in service until VJ-Day Operationally, it was used best from an advantage in altitude, speed and position. The basic combat tactic was simple: one pass and haul ass. If they began with a 2,000 ft (610 m) altitude advantage, P-40s could make four passes through an enemy formation before having to leave the fight to climb back to the perch again. Defensive tactics were to split-S quickly and dive down to gain speed and pull away. An alternate was to turn into the enemy or, if at low altitude, to skid violently. When production ended in December 1944, the US Army had accepted 12,302 of them, the third largest number of fighters built for World War II. They cost, by then, $60,552 apiece.

Republic P-47 Thunderbolt: after a couple of false starts which cost almost a year's time, Republic's proposal for a new fighter was accepted in mid-1940. Orders for production aircraft followed, and the first prototype flew on 6 May 1941. In April 1943 the Thunderbolt entered combat. 'She really can dive!' said one startled pilot. 'She'd damn well better,' said his commander, 'she sure as Hell can't climb!' The P-47 escorted bombers for a while in Europe, until the P-51 came along. And then it found its true role as a powerful fighter-bomber. In deep interdiction strikes against rail and road targets, it destroyed thousands of locomotives, railway rolling stock, trucks, tanks and other vehicles. Overall kill ratio was almost five to one. The US Army bought a total of 15,686 of them, more than any other fighter, and by the war's end they were costing the taxpayer $83,000 apiece.

This particularly attractive colour scheme identified the P-51D Mustangs of the 4th FS, 52nd FG. This outfit served with the 15th Air Force, and finished the war operating from Torretto and Piagiolino, Italy.

North American P-51B Mustang of the 37th Fighter Sqn, 361st Fighter Group, 8th Air Force, based at Bottisham, England, 1944.

American Fighters of World War II

North American A-36 attack Mustang with Allison engine, of the 27th Fighter Bomber Group on the Italian front, 1944. Note the 190 mission symbols.

North American P-51B Mustang of the 487th Fighter Sqn, 352nd Fighter Group, based at Bodney, England, 1944.

The F-6 series were dedicated reconnaissance aircraft of the USAAF, originally converted from fighters. This F-6B was a converted P-51A, with four wing guns and two K-24 cameras in the fuselage. This example served with the 9th Air Force's 107th Tac Recon Sqn, and has a Malcolm hood.

North American P-51 Mustang: if it had not been for the UK's desperate need for fighters, the Mustang might never have been born. And once born, the USAAF did almost everything it could to avoid looking at it. Designed in 1940 in response to a British request, the prototype NA-73 first flew 26 October 1940. It featured use of a daringly different NACA 'low-drag, laminar-flow' aerofoil section, but there are doubts that the Mustang often achieved either characteristic in service. Nevertheless, it became an exceptional fighter after its sleek airframe was married to the British Rolls-Royce Merlin engine. In the new guise, finally bought by the USAAF, it became the fighter par excellence, escorting bombers to Berlin and beyond, hammering at ground targets in glide-bombing attacks, and tangling with the best the Luftwaffe could put up, including jets and even the rocket-propelled Me 163. The US Army purchased 14,068 of them, second only in quantity to the P-47. In 1945, you could buy a Mustang for $50,985.

Taken in early 1944, this fine picture of a P-51D shows the underwing racks for drop tanks (or bombs). The Millie P flew with the 343rd FS, 55th FG with yellow/green nose and spinner, olive drab rear and yellow rudder.

North American P-51 Mustang

Though it was in service only in the final 18 months of World War II, the P-51D and basically identical P-51K (different propeller) have since hogged almost all the Mustang limelight and also accounted for most of the 15,586 of all models produced. This aircraft, USAAF 1944–13926, served with the 361st Fighter Group of the 8th Air Force, at Bottisham (England) and in late 1944 at St. Dizier (France).

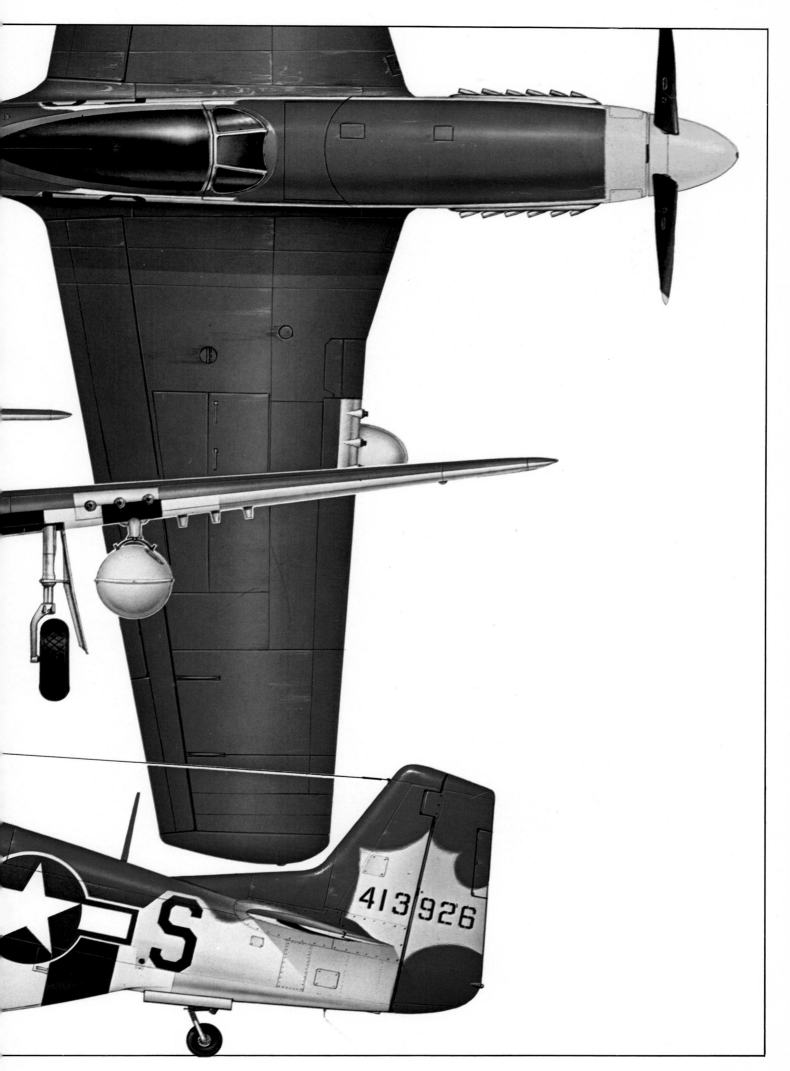

The Army Attackers

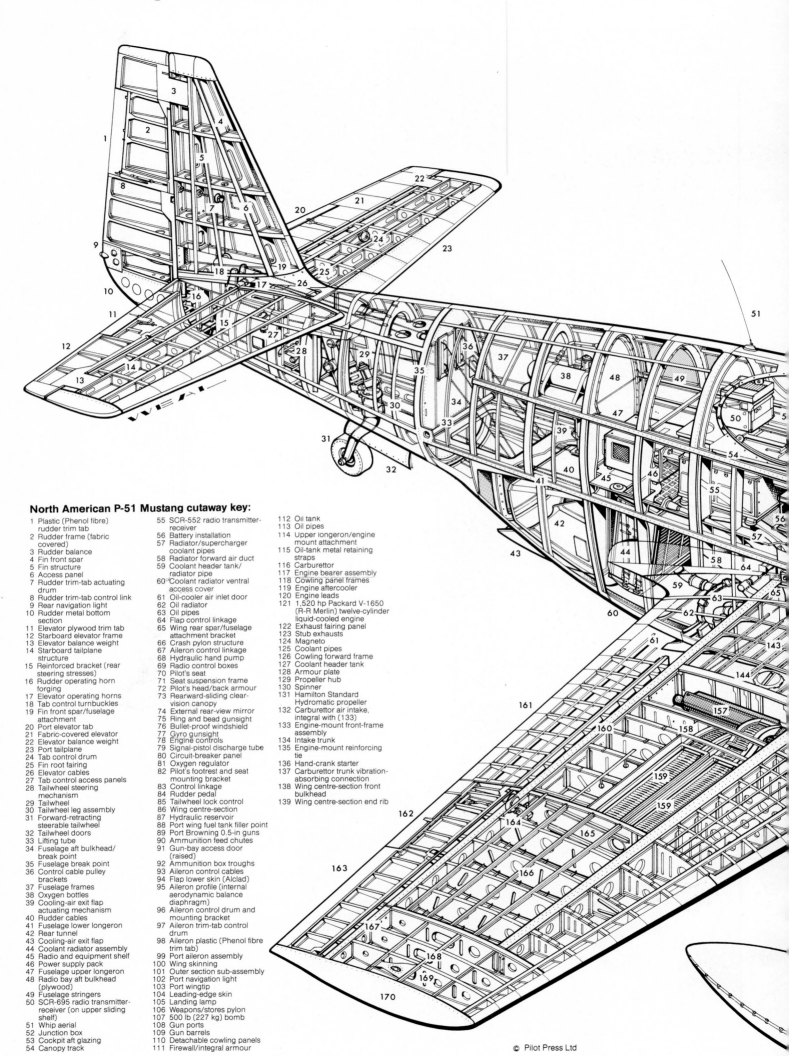

North American P-51 Mustang cutaway key:

1 Plastic (Phenol fibre) rudder trim tab
2 Rudder frame (fabric covered)
3 Rudder balance
4 Fin front spar
5 Fin structure
6 Access panel
7 Rudder trim-tab actuating drum
8 Rudder trim-tab control link
9 Rear navigation light
10 Rudder metal bottom section
11 Elevator plywood trim tab
12 Starboard elevator frame
13 Elevator balance weight
14 Starboard tailplane structure
15 Reinforced bracket (rear steering stresses)
16 Rudder operating horn forging
17 Elevator operating horns
18 Tab control turnbuckles
19 Fin front spar/fuselage attachment
20 Port elevator tab
21 Fabric-covered elevator
22 Elevator balance weight
23 Port tailplane
24 Tab control drum
25 Fin root fairing
26 Elevator cables
27 Tab control access panels
28 Tailwheel steering mechanism
29 Tailwheel
30 Tailwheel leg assembly
31 Forward-retracting steerable tailwheel
32 Tailwheel doors
33 Lifting tube
34 Fuselage aft bulkhead/break point
35 Fuselage break point
36 Control cable pulley brackets
37 Fuselage frames
38 Oxygen bottles
39 Cooling-air exit flap actuating mechanism
40 Rudder cables
41 Fuselage lower longeron
42 Rear tunnel
43 Cooling-air exit flap
44 Coolant radiator assembly
45 Radio and equipment shelf
46 Power supply pack
47 Fuselage upper longeron
48 Radio bay aft bulkhead (plywood)
49 Fuselage stringers
50 SCR-695 radio transmitter-receiver (on upper sliding shelf)
51 Whip aerial
52 Junction box
53 Cockpit aft glazing
54 Canopy track
55 SCR-552 radio transmitter-receiver
56 Battery installation
57 Radiator/supercharger coolant pipes
58 Radiator forward air duct
59 Coolant header tank/radiator pipe
60 Coolant radiator ventral access cover
61 Oil-cooler air inlet door
62 Oil radiator
63 Oil pipes
64 Flap control linkage
65 Wing rear spar/fuselage attachment bracket
66 Crash pylon structure
67 Aileron control linkage
68 Hydraulic hand pump
69 Radio control boxes
70 Pilot's seat
71 Seat suspension frame
72 Pilot's head/back armour
73 Rearward-sliding clear-vision canopy
74 External rear-view mirror
75 Ring and bead gunsight
76 Bullet-proof windshield
77 Gyro gunsight
78 Engine controls
79 Signal-pistol discharge tube
80 Circuit-breaker panel
81 Oxygen regulator
82 Pilot's footrest and seat mounting bracket
83 Control linkage
84 Rudder pedal
85 Tailwheel lock control
86 Wing centre-section
87 Hydraulic reservoir
88 Port wing fuel tank filler point
89 Port Browning 0.5-in guns
90 Ammunition feed chutes
91 Gun-bay access door (raised)
92 Ammunition box troughs
93 Aileron control cables
94 Flap lower skin (Alclad)
95 Aileron profile (internal aerodynamic balance diaphragm)
96 Aileron control drum and mounting bracket
97 Aileron trim-tab control drum
98 Aileron plastic (Phenol fibre trim tab)
99 Port aileron assembly
100 Wing skinning
101 Outer section sub-assembly
102 Port navigation light
103 Port wingtip
104 Leading-edge skin
105 Landing lamp
106 Weapons/stores pylon
107 500 lb (227 kg) bomb
108 Gun ports
109 Gun barrels
110 Detachable cowling panels
111 Firewall/integral armour
112 Oil tank
113 Oil pipes
114 Upper longeron/engine mount attachment
115 Oil-tank metal retaining straps
116 Carburettor
117 Engine bearer assembly
118 Cowling panel frames
119 Engine aftercooler
120 Engine leads
121 1,520 hp Packard V-1650 (R-R Merlin) twelve-cylinder liquid-cooled engine
122 Exhaust fairing panel
123 Stub exhausts
124 Magneto
125 Coolant pipes
126 Cowling forward frame
127 Coolant header tank
128 Armour plate
129 Propeller hub
130 Spinner
131 Hamilton Standard Hydromatic propeller
132 Carburettor air intake, integral with (133)
133 Engine-mount front-frame assembly
134 Intake trunk
135 Engine-mount reinforcing tie
136 Hand-crank starter
137 Carburettor trunk vibration-absorbing connection
138 Wing centre-section front bulkhead
139 Wing centre-section end rib

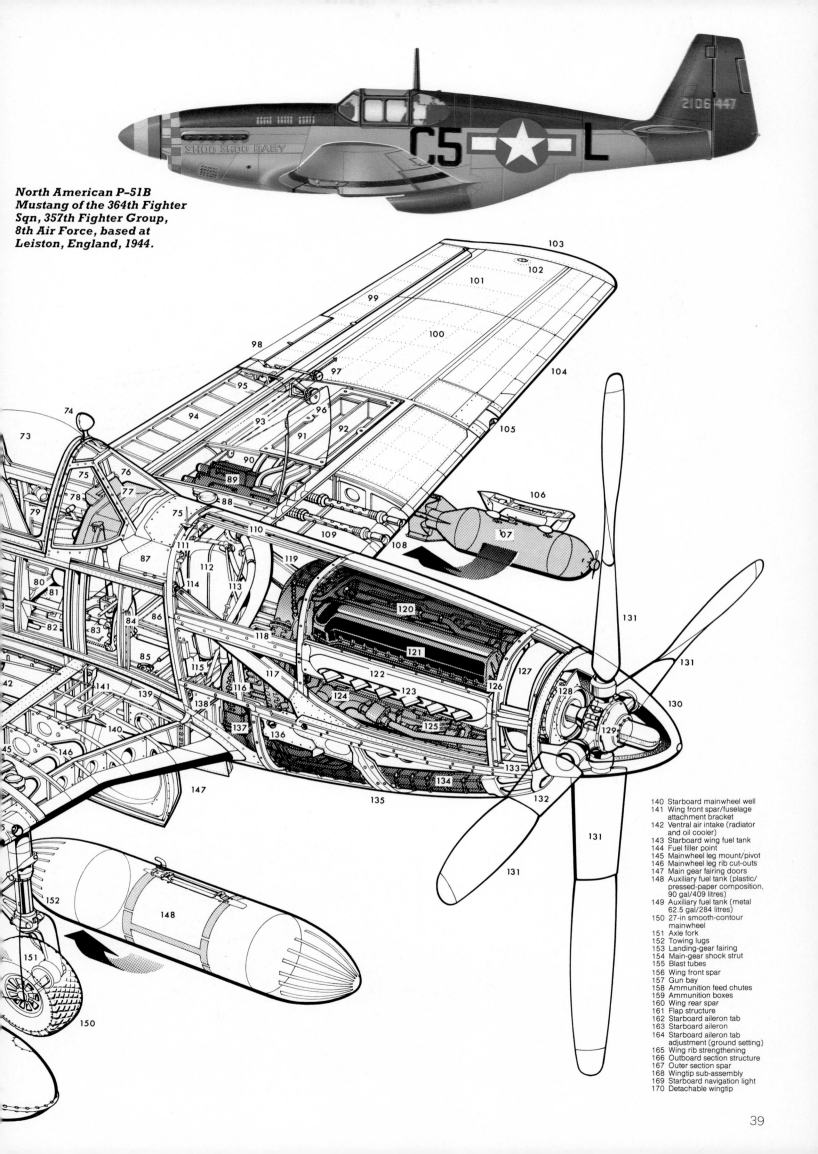

*North American P-51B
Mustang of the 364th Fighter
Sqn, 357th Fighter Group,
8th Air Force, based at
Leiston, England, 1944.*

140 Starboard mainwheel well
141 Wing front spar/fuselage
    attachment bracket
142 Ventral air intake (radiator
    and oil cooler)
143 Starboard wing fuel tank
144 Fuel filler point
145 Mainwheel leg mount/pivot
146 Mainwheel leg rib cut-outs
147 Main gear fairing doors
148 Auxiliary fuel tank (plastic/
    pressed-paper composition,
    90 gal/409 litres)
149 Auxiliary fuel tank (metal
    62.5 gal/284 litres)
150 27-in smooth-contour
    mainwheel
151 Axle fork
152 Towing lugs
153 Landing-gear fairing
154 Main-gear shock strut
155 Blast tubes
156 Wing front spar
157 Gun bay
158 Ammunition feed chutes
159 Ammunition boxes
160 Wing rear spar
161 Flap structure
162 Starboard aileron tab
163 Starboard aileron
164 Starboard aileron tab
    adjustment (ground setting)
165 Wing rib strengthening
166 Outboard section structure
167 Outer section spar
168 Wingtip sub-assembly
169 Starboard navigation light
170 Detachable wingtip

Pacific Pugilists

The US Navy at first fielded some forlorn types, initially holding its own with the Grumman F4F. Then came two all-time greats, the Hellcat and Corsair that swept all before them.

A Hellcat recovers aboard its carrier in the Pacific. This aircraft more than any other was to turn the tide against the Japanese aggressors after the psychological and physical devastation of Pearl Harbor.

Taken on 18 June 1944 this dramatic photograph shows a flaming J1N1, possibly operating in the suicide role.

If there were any lingering prejudices against the effectiveness of air power in the minds of high-level US Navy officers, they were erased at one stroke by the stunning Japanese attack on Pearl Harbor on the morning of 7 December 1941. The US Navy's principal Pacific base was devastated, and the bulk of its capital ships—proud battleships with the entire tradition of the US Navy behind them—was destroyed.

The US Navy was forced to fight its war with carriers, the only capital ships left. But it was a pitifully small force that faced a preponderance of Japanese naval strength. In the Pacific, the US Navy had two carriers, neither near Pearl Harbor. The USS *Enterprise* was returning from a ferry run to Wake Island, having just delivered the doomed Marine Fighting Squadron (VMF) 211, with a dozen Grumman F4F-3 Wildcats as complement. She carried her own fighter force of 18 Wildcats. The USS *Lexington* was headed for Midway Island, to deliver a Marine scout

Pacific Pugilists

bomber squadron. She was defended by 18 Brewster F2A-3s.

The USS *Ranger, Wasp* and *Yorktown* were on station in the Atlantic, with a total complement of 90 Grumman F4Fs. The USS *Hornet* also was in Atlantic waters on her shakedown cruise; she had been commissioned two months before. Her fighters were 18 Wildcats. The USS *Saratoga* was lying at anchor in San Diego harbour, having just come out of overhaul.

Two carriers with 36 fighters, plus 12 Wildcats on Wake Island, faced the Japanese attack in the Pacific. It was one of the two wars, both different, that the United States Navy waged. In the Atlantic, the campaign was to be one of blockade and protection of shipping, plus participation in three future amphibious assaults (North Africa, southern France and Normandy). In the Pacific, the objectives were to stop the Japanese drive, and then to roll it back to the home islands.

No information is available on this F4F–3A squadron beyond the fact the date was 12 May 1942. Despite its narrow track the F4F was adequately stable on a pitching deck. Note SBDs in the rear.

The new weapon

Distance and time were to work in favour of the United States, so that the arsenal of democracy could get production lines moving at a high volume. Early Japanese conquests, which seemed absolutely overwhelming when first studied, placed their forces out at the ends of a number of thin supply lines that were vulnerable to sea and air attack. Cut them, even one at a time, and Japan would begin to feel defeat.

The US Navy had an ace in the hole: radar. Close co-operation and technology transfer with the British had been naval policy for several years before the war, and the basic concepts of shipboard use of radar had been explored and developed by December 1941. During 1940, the US Navy had been conducting experiments with ship-based search radar, and *Yorktown*

This F4F-4 of squadron VF-41 was embarked aboard USS Ranger in early 1942. On 15 May 1942 the order went out erasing the red centre of the national insignia, for obvious reasons.

Brewster Buffalo

SPECIFICATION
Type: single-seat land- or ship-based fighter
Powerplant: (F2A-3) one 1,200-hp (895-kW) Wright R-1820-40 Cyclone radial piston engine
Performance: maximum speed 321 mph (517 km/h) at 16,500 ft (5030 m); cruising speed 258 mph (415 km/h); service ceiling 33,200 ft (10120 m); range 965 miles (1553 km)
Weights: empty 4,732 lb (2146 kg); maximum take-off 7,159 lb (3247 kg)
Dimensions: span 35 ft 0 in (10.67 m); length 26 ft 4 in (8.03 m); height 12 ft 1 in (3.68 m); wing area 208.9 sq ft (19.41 m²)
Armament: four 0.50-in (12.7-mm) machine-guns, plus two 100-lb (45-kg) bombs

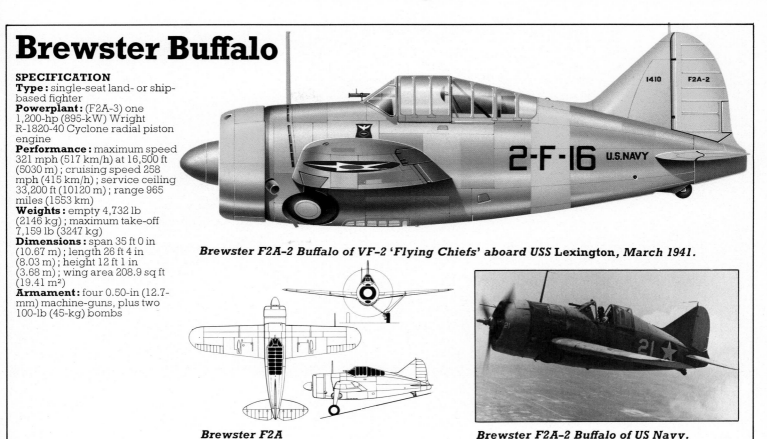

Brewster F2A-2 Buffalo of VF-2 'Flying Chiefs' aboard USS Lexington, *March 1941.*

Brewster F2A

Brewster F2A-2 Buffalo of US Navy.

had reported successfully detecting and tracking aircraft as far as 100 miles (161 km) distant. In July 1941 the US Navy approved the construction of radar plots (the equivalent of the later combat intelligence centres) for carriers, and started on the first aboard the *Hornet*. Within two weeks, the Chief of Naval Operations ordered that fighter direction centres be established on all carriers.

Ironically, it was the Navy among US services that first put Claire Chennault's basic concepts of air defence into operation. The ships had radar, the basic means of detection, and radar plots, which were a method of reporting information. That information was used by the fighter director

Taken on 3 August 1942, this peel-off by F2A-2 fighters (never officially named Buffalo in US service) took place at a training unit in the United States. By that time no F2As were left in front-line US service, the last being with the USAAF in Australia.

Pacific Pugilists

to vector combat elements to intercept the incoming threat. Once in sight of their targets, it was left to the fighters to apply their team tactics and to destroy the enemy aircraft.

Less than two months after the attack at Pearl Harbor, the US Navy steamed its first carrier offensive westward to the Gilbert and Marshall Islands. Two task forces, with their flagships *Enterprise* and *Yorktown,* raided those islands, and then went on to hit Wake and Marcus Islands. More carrier strikes hit Japanese shipping that was supporting landings at Lae and Salamaua, on New Guinea. And then the first of many sea-air battles erupted in the Coral Sea. Neither side's ships ever saw each other, the fight was a series of air attacks. The Japanese were frustrated in their attempt to land troops at Port Moresby, New Guinea, the US Navy lost the *Lexington.*

The key battle developed off Midway island in June 1942. There, the Japanese lost control of

Perhaps the greatest piston-engined fighter of all, the F4U Corsair took a long time to develop. Some of the first went to the famed VF-17

One of a series of air-to-air colour shots secured during manufacturer's testing of an F6F-3 Hellcat over Long Island.

More than any other single type it was the F6F that defeated Japan in the skies. This F6F-3 has just recovered aboard the famed USS Hornet in June 1944, and appears swept-back as deck crew fold the wings.

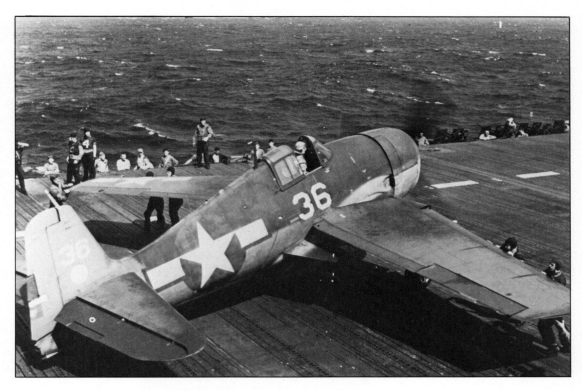

Greatest single war-winner over the Japanese aviators was the F6F, which though started much later than the F4U was in action by 1943 in greater numbers. Here F6F-3s start Double Wasp engines aboard USS Yorktown, the first being (it is believed) the first F6F to join the Fleet.

the air, their fighters and bombers hammered out of the sky by Grumman Wildcats. It was the turning point of the naval war in the Pacific. The *Yorktown* was abandoned after attack, but the Japanese lost four carriers and, more importantly, the best of their pilots. From then on, Japanese pilot quality was markedly inferior to its level earlier in the war.

In August, the long campaign to seize and hold Guadalcanal began, and during subsequent naval battles, four US carriers—the entire Pacific fleet strength—were put out of service. *Enterprise* was bombed 24 August and *Saratoga* was damaged a week later by a torpedo; both left the theatre for repairs. *Wasp* was sunk by a submarine 15 September, and *Hornet* was lost to air attack on 26 October. Meantime, *Enterprise* had been repaired and had returned to become the only carrier in the Pacific one year after war came to the United States.

As in legends, the US Marines came to the rescue. With their new Vought F4U Corsairs they

Vought F4U Corsair

The most famous of all Corsairs, this F4U–1A was flown by Lt Ira C. 'Ike' Kepford, the US Navy's leading ace in the Pacific, in early 1944. His 16 victories are recorded by Rising (he would say 'setting') Suns. He was one of 15 aces in the first Navy squadron to go to war with the F4U, VF–17 (Lt–Cdr Tommy Blackburn).

Pacific Pugilists

Vought F4U Corsair cutaway drawing key

1 Spinner
2 Three-blade Hamilton Standard constant-speed propeller
3 Reduction gear housing
4 Nose ring
5 Pratt & Whitney R-2800-8 Double Wasp 18-cylinder two-row engine
6 Exhaust pipes
7 Hydraulically-operated cowling
8 Fixed cowling panels
9 Wing leading-edge unprotected integral fuel tank, capacity 62 US gal (235 litres)
10 Truss-type main spar
11 Leading-edge rib structure
12 Starboard navigation light
13 Wingtip
14 Wing structure
15 Wing ribs
16 Wing outer-section (fabric skinning aft of main spar)
17 Starboard aileron
18 Ammunition boxes (max total capacity 2,350 rounds)
19 Aileron trim tab
20 Aerial mast
21 Forward bulkhead
22 Oil tank, capacity 26 US gal (98 litres)

23 Oil tank forward armour plate
24 Fire suppressor cylinder
25 Supercharger housing
26 Exhaust trunking
27 Blower assembly
28 Engine support frame
29 Engine control runs
30 Wing mainspar carry-through structure
31 Engine support attachment
32 Upper cowling deflection plate (0.1 in/0.25 cm aluminium)
33 Fuel filler cap
34 Fuselage main fuel tank, capacity 237 US gal (897 litres)
35 Upper longeron
36 Fuselage forward frames
37 Rudder pedals
38 Heelboards
39 Control column
40 Instrument panel
41 Reflector sight
42 Armour-glass windshield
43 Rear-view mirror
44 Rearward-sliding cockpit canopy
45 Handgrip
46 Headrest
47 Pilot's head and back armour
48 Canopy frame
49 Pilot's seat

50 Engine control quadrant
51 Trim tab control wheels
52 Wing-folding lever
53 Centre/aft fuselage bulkhead
54 Radio shelf
55 Radio installation
56 Canopy track
57 Bulkhead
58 Aerial lead-in
59 Aerial mast
60 Aerials
61 Heavy-sheet skin plating
62 Dorsal identification light
63 Longeron
64 Control runs
65 Aft fuselage structure
66 Compass installation
67 Lifting tube
68 Access/inspection panels
69 Fin/fuselage forward attachment
70 Starboard tailplane
71 Elevator balance
72 Fin structure
73 Inspection panels
74 Rudder balance
75 Aerial stub
76 Rudder upper hinge
77 Rudder structure
78 Diagonal bracing
79 Rudder trim tab
80 Trim tab actuating rod

81 Access panel
82 Rudder post
83 Tailplane end rib
84 Elevator control runs
85 Fixed fairing root
86 Elevator trim tabs (port and starboard)
87 Tail cone
88 Rear navigation light
89 Port elevator
90 Elevator balance
91 Port tailplane structure
92 Arrester hook (stowed)
93 Tail section frames
94 Fairing
95 Tailwheel (retracted)
96 Arrester hook (lowered)
97 Tailwheel/hook doors
98 Tailwheel/hook attachment/pivot
99 Mooring/tie-down lug
100 Rearward-retracting tailwheel
101 Tailwheel oleo
102 Support strut
103 Arrester hook actuating strut
104 Aft/tail section bulkhead
105 Arrester hook shock-absorber
106 Tailwheel/arrester hook cylinder
107 Tailwheel retraction strut
108 Bulkhead attachment points
109 Fuselage skinning
110 Bulkhead frame

111 Elevator/rudder control runs
112 Entry hand/foothold
113 Hydraulically-operated flap inboard section
114 Wing fold line
115 'Flap gap' closure plate
116 Hydraulically-operated flap outboard section
117 Aileron balance tab (port only)
118 Aileron trim tab
119 Port aileron
120 Deck-landing grip
121 Port wingtip
122 Port navigation light
123 Pitot head
124 Leading-edge ribs
125 Wing outer-section structure
126 Ammunition boxes
127 Three 0.5-in (12.7-mm) Colt-Browning M2 wing machine guns with 400 rpg (inboard pair) and 375 rpg (outboard)
128 Wing fold outboard cylinder
129 Wing leading-edge unprotected integral fuel tank, capacity 62 US gal (235 litres) — deleted from final 150 Corsair IIs
130 Machine gun blast tubes
131 Mainwheel retraction strut
132 Torque links
133 Port mainwheel
134 Axle

135 Mainwheel leg fairing
136 Mainwheel oleo leg
137 Mainwheel leg pivot point
138 Undercarriage main spar attachment
139 Undercarriage actuating cylinder
140 Main spar fold point
141 Mainwheel well
142 Contoured main spar inboard section
143 All-aluminium wing centre-section
144 Main spar/fuselage attachment
145 Blower radiator
146 Oil cooler
147 Engine supercharger intake duct
148 Exhaust stacks
149 Engine supercharger air intake
150 Auxiliary fuel tank centre-line attachment points
151 'Duramold' auxiliary drop-tank, capacity 175 US gal (662 litres)
152 Bomb attachment shackle (underwing inner section, F4U-1D and Corsair II only)
153 Bomb load, up to 1,000 lb (454 kg) each side (F4U-1D and Corsair II only)

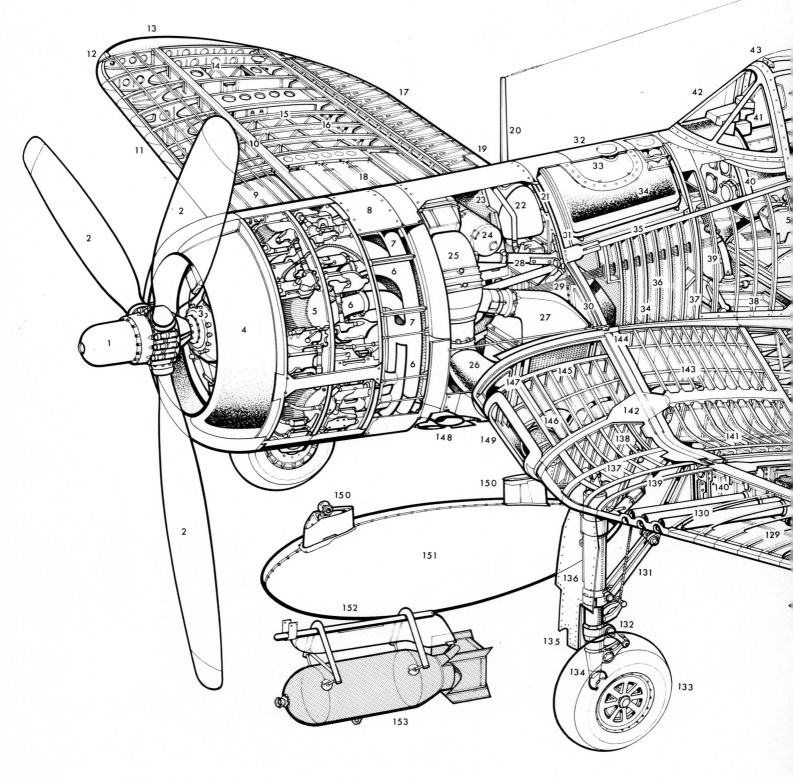

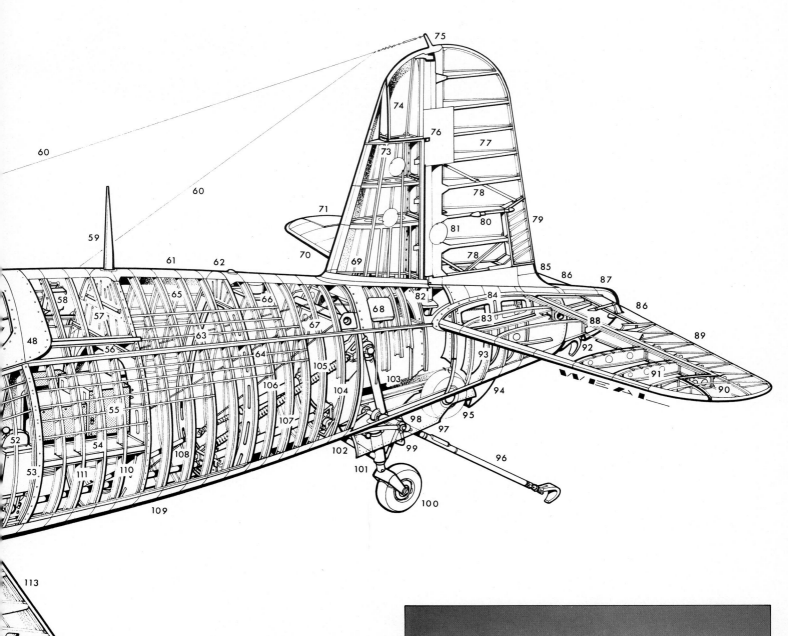

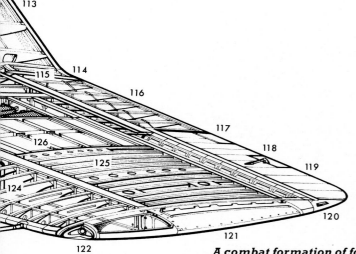

A combat formation of four Vought F4U-1 Corsair fighters (two two-ship elements) of the celebrated US Marine Corps 'Black Sheep' squadron (VMF-124) bank left over the island of Bougainville in the Solomons group. Operating in such an archipelago, the Corsair soon proved a potent and versatile fighter-bomber.

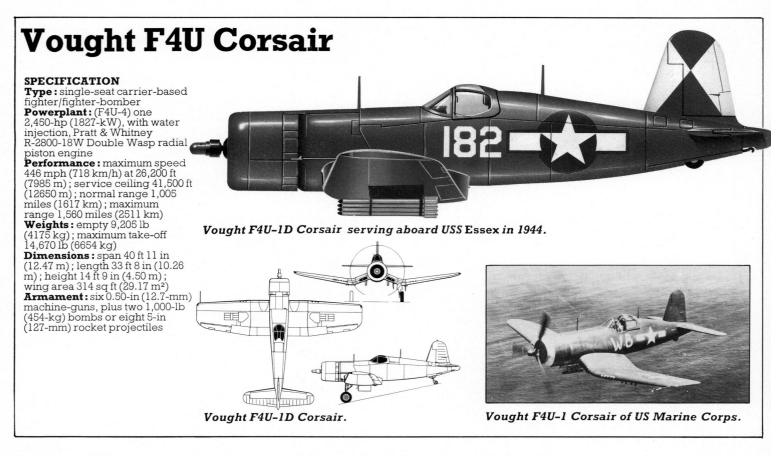

Vought F4U Corsair

SPECIFICATION
Type: single-seat carrier-based fighter/fighter-bomber
Powerplant: (F4U-4) one 2,450-hp (1827-kW), with water injection, Pratt & Whitney R-2800-18W Double Wasp radial piston engine
Performance: maximum speed 446 mph (718 km/h) at 26,200 ft (7985 m); service ceiling 41,500 ft (12650 m); normal range 1,005 miles (1617 km); maximum range 1,560 miles (2511 km)
Weights: empty 9,205 lb (4175 kg); maximum take-off 14,670 lb (6654 kg)
Dimensions: span 40 ft 11 in (12.47 m); length 33 ft 8 in (10.26 m); height 14 ft 9 in (4.50 m); wing area 314 sq ft (29.17 m²)
Armament: six 0.50-in (12.7-mm) machine-guns, plus two 1,000-lb (454-kg) bombs or eight 5-in (127-mm) rocket projectiles

Vought F4U-1D Corsair serving aboard USS Essex in 1944.

Vought F4U-1D Corsair.

Vought F4U-1 Corsair of US Marine Corps.

operated out of land bases in the Solomons chain, honing the tactics and manoeuvres that made the F4U into a deadly killing machine. Their continuous fighting, shared with US Army Air Force units, first held the Japanese at bay and then drove them out of island after island.

New strike force

In August 1943 the US Navy played another ace: the Grumman F6F-3 Hellcat. Rugged, heavily armed, manned by a fresh crop of well-trained pilots and based on a rapidly increasing number of new and fast carriers of the 'Essex' and 'Independence' classes, the Hellcats became the spearhead of a new naval strength. The mobile, powerful fast carrier strike force of air and surface groups was born.

In this new teaming of naval arms, the fighter grew in importance, reflected in the change in aircraft complement approved in October 1943. It raised fighter numbers aboard 'Essex'-class carriers to 36, equal to bomber strength and twice that of the torpedo planes.

Two years after war began, the US Navy was able to assemble fast carrier task forces around

Home of the 'Black Sheep', the most famous of all US Marine fighter squadrons. VMF-214 was then (11 September 1943) based at Espiritu Santo, New Hebrides, and leading his men out to their F4U-1s is 'Pappy' Boyington himself.

By far the most important operators of the Corsair in World War II were the fighter squadrons of the US Marine Corps, based on island airstrips in the Pacific. This bombing mission was photographed leaving parking areas on Majuro Atoll, in the Marshalls, on 29 August 1944. The squadron belongs to the 4th Marine Air Wing.

new carriers. In January 1944, when raids were begun to support the occupation of the Marshall Islands, Task Force 58 sailed in four groups including six heavy and six light carriers. Six months later, TF 58 steamed against the Marianas with seven heavy and eight light carriers. In that campaign, US Navy air power scored its greatest victory: the 'great Marianas turkey shoot'.

The greatest battle

It was the largest naval air battle in history. The antagonists were about equal in air strength at the start: approximately 1,000 Japanese planes and pilots faced about 1,100 Americans. But when it was over, the US held the Philippine Sea and the sky above it, and had hammered the Japanese so fiercely that there was no possibility of their recovery. Only 35 aircraft remained operational in their fleet; the rest were lost to American action, either shot out of the sky, at the bottom with their sunken carriers, or damaged beyond repair. Three Japanese carriers were sunk, and another pair had been hit too badly to regain capability for action. The greatest Japanese loss was among the aircrews. More than three-quarters of the Japanese naval airmen in that battle never went back home. It was the end of Japan's naval air arm; there were no reserves, and no filled pipeline of trained pilots.

Within two months after that great air battle, the fighter complement was raised again to 54, this time outnumbering both the bomber strength of 24 aircraft and the torpedo plane strength of 18.

The war rolled on. Landings in southern France were supported by US carrier air teams. The Philippines were invaded and occupied, as the Japanese continued their retreat. Task Force 38

With its radar pod out of sight on the far wing this F4U-2 served with US Marine night-fighter squadron VMF(N)-532. It was based at Roi island, Kwajalein Atoll, in 1943-44, and was flown by the CO, Major Everett H. Vaughan.

Pacific Pugilists

The family resemblance is obvious between the F6F-3 Hellcats on the right (on the port side of the deck of this escort carrier) and the TBF Avenger torpedo-bombers in the foreground. The flat-top was USS Monterey, seen in January 1944.

used 17 carriers in its pre-invasion assault on Leyte; an additional 18 escort carriers supplied air support for the landing itself. And again the fighter complement increased, this time to 73 for the 'Essex'-class ships, against 15 each of the bombers and torpedo planes. The US Marines came aboard in December 1944 with fighter squadrons, and in January fighter-bomber squadrons were established.

Japan held on tenaciously, while the carriers steamed inexorably westward. In July 1945 Task Force 38 began air strikes against Japan from Hokkaido in the north to Kyushu in the south. Hellcats bombed and strafed, rocketed ground targets, shot down the occasional interceptor, and escorted the bombers. It was a one-sided affair, with light US Navy losses and tremendous damage done to the Japanese. The war was lost, and had the Japanese admitted the fact the bombs at Hiroshima and Nagasaki might not have been necessary.

Rapid-fire catapult launches from the fleet carrier USS Randolph as F6Fs are hurled skyward for a strike on the Japanese mainland in July 1945. Underwing rockets are almost all hidden by the lowered flaps.

Grumman F6F Hellcat

SPECIFICATION
Type: single-seat carrier-based fighter/fighter-bomber
Powerplant: (F6F-5) one 2,000-hp (1491-kW) Pratt & Whitney R-2800-10W Double Wasp radial piston engine
Performance: maximum speed 380 mph (612 km/h) at 23,400 ft (7130 m); cruising speed 168 mph (270 km/h); service ceiling 37,300 ft (11370 m); range with a 150-US gallon (568-litre) drop tank 1,530 miles (2462 km)
Weights: empty 9,153 lb (4152 kg); maximum take-off 15,413 lb (6991 kg)
Dimensions: span 42 ft 10 in (13.06 m); length 33 ft 7 in (10.24 m); height 13 ft 6 in (4.11 m); wing area 334 sq ft (31.03 m²)
Armament: six 0.50-in (12.7-mm) machine-guns (some late models had two machine-guns replaced by 20-mm cannon), plus two 1,000-lb (454-kg) bombs, or six 5-in (127-mm) rocket projectiles

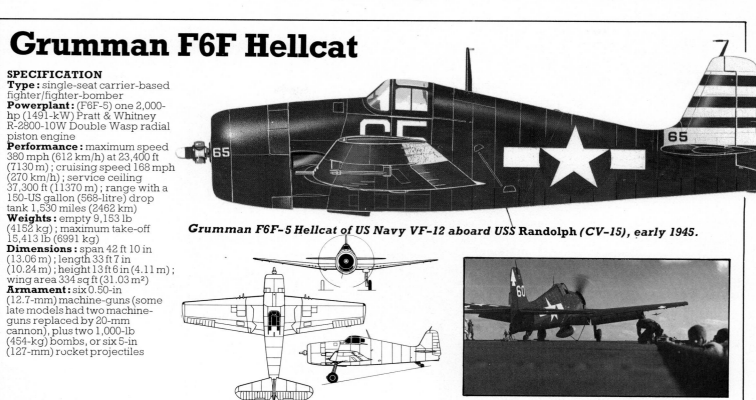

Grumman F6F-5 Hellcat of US Navy VF-12 aboard USS Randolph (CV-15), early 1945.

Grumman F6F-3 Hellcat.

Grumman F6F Hellcat launching from USS Randolph.

The final devastation of Japan and its once-sprawling network of bases and sea lanes had been hastened by powerful air forces available on mobile bases of the fleet. And for the last year and more of the war, the predominant component of that air force was the fighter.

Naval fighter sketches

Grumman F4F Wildcat: although it was the first-line strength in the Pacific and Atlantic when war came, the Wildcat was phased out of that role by the Hellcat and the Corsair. Built in great quantities by both Grumman and General Motors (as the FM series), the tubby fighters served on more than 100 escort carriers, protecting convoys in the wild waters of the North Atlantic, or supporting amphibious landings in the Pacific with rockets, bombs and gunnery. Final kill ratio was 7:1. The US Navy accepted 7,415 of all models, F4F and FM.

Grumman F6F Hellcat: big brother of the Wildcat, the Hellcat was defined on 15 January 1941. Construction was ordered 30 June 1941 and the first XF6F-1 flew 26 June 1942. Deliveries of the production F6F-3 version began 3 October 1942 and by August 1943 the

Another deck filled with products from the 'Grumman Ironworks', TBFs on the left and F6Fs on the right. The Hellcats are carrying drop tanks and are probably on an escort mission, without bombs or rockets.

Grumman F6F Hellcat

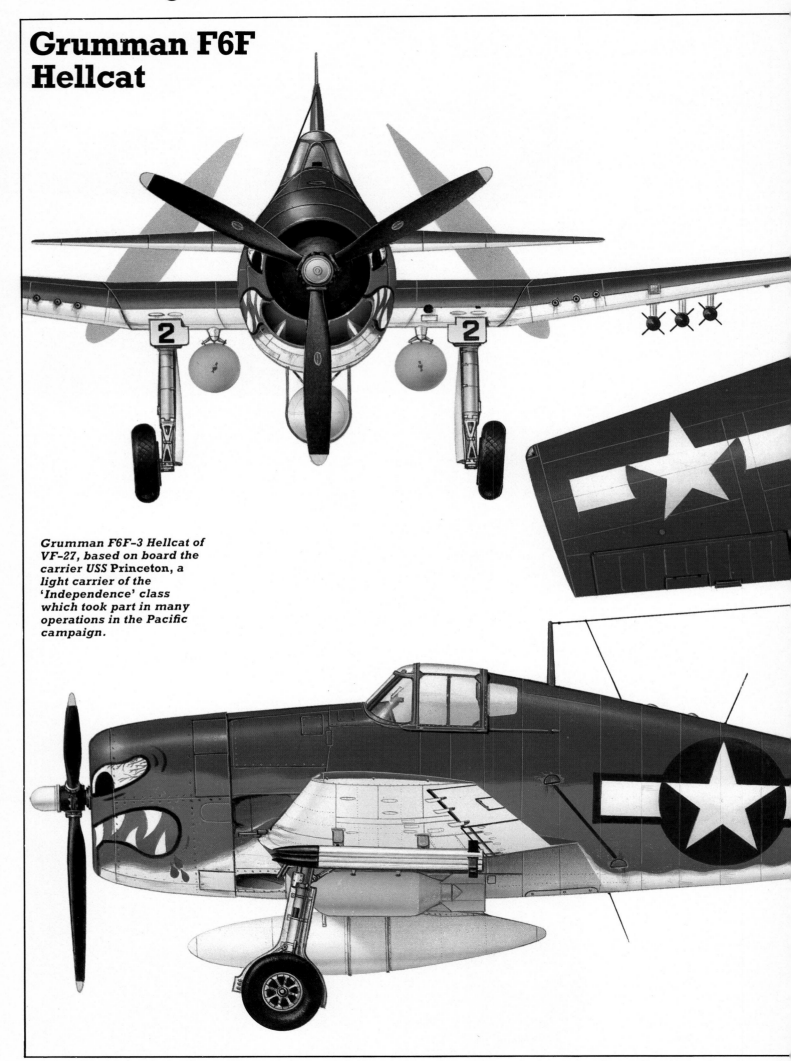

Grumman F6F-3 Hellcat of VF-27, based on board the carrier USS Princeton, a light carrier of the 'Independence' class which took part in many operations in the Pacific campaign.

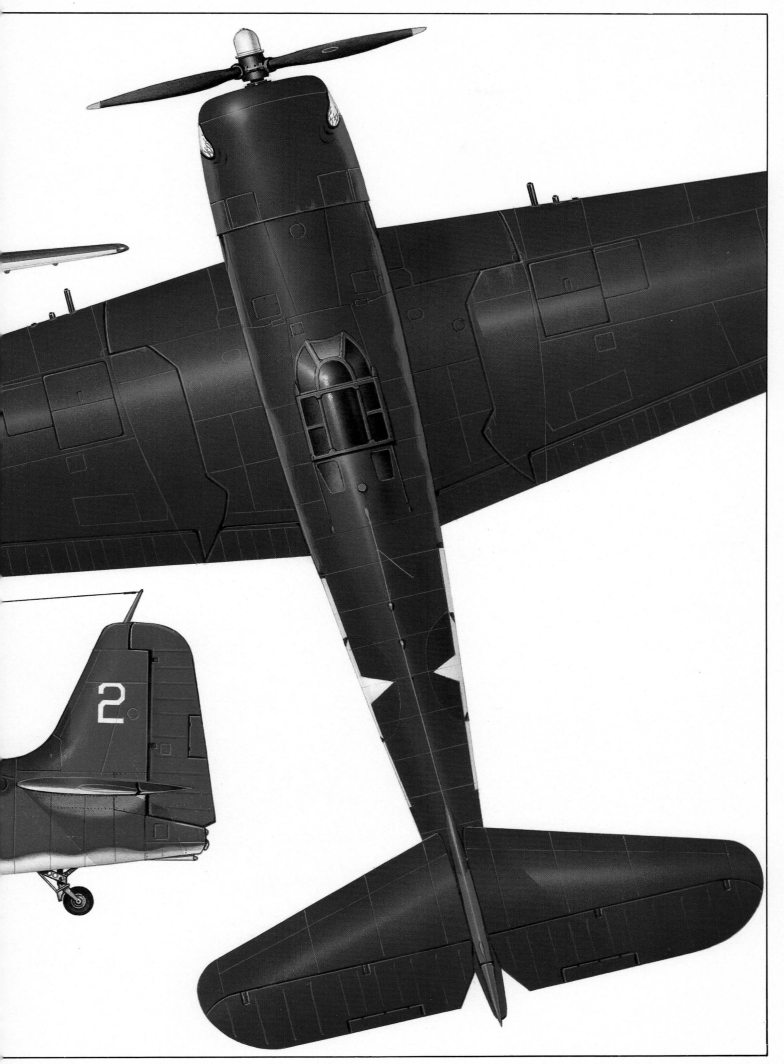

Pacific Pugilists

Grumman F6F-5 Hellcat cutaway drawing key

1 Radio mast
2 Rudder balance
3 Rudder upper hinge
4 Aluminium alloy fin ribs
5 Rudder post
6 Rudder structure
7 Rudder trim tab
8 Rudder middle hinge
9 Diagonal stiffeners
10 Aluminium alloy elevator trim tab
11 Fabric-covered (and taped) elevator surfaces
12 Elevator balance
13 Flush riveted leading-edge strip
14 Arrester hook (extended)
15 Tailplane ribs
16 Tail navigation (running) light
17 Rudder lower hinge
18 Arrester hook (stowed)
19 Fin main spar lower cut-out
20 Tailplane end rib
21 Fin forward spar
22 Fuselage/fin root fairing
23 Port elevator
24 Aluminium alloy-skinned tailplane
25 Section light
26 Fuselage aft frame
27 Control access
28 Bulkhead
29 Tailwheel hydraulic shock-absorber
30 Tailwheel centring mechanism
31 Tailwheel steel mounting arm

32 Rearward-retracting tailwheel (hard rubber tyre)
33 Fairing
34 Steel plate door fairing
35 Tricing sling support tube
36 Hydraulic actuating cylinder
37 Flanged ring fuselage frames
38 Control cable runs
39 Fuselage longerons
40 Relay box
41 Dorsal rod antenna
42 Dorsal recognition light
43 Radio aerial
44 Radio mast
45 Aerial lead-in
46 Dorsal frame stiffeners
47 Junction box
48 Radio equipment (upper rack)
49 Radio shelf
50 Control cable runs
51 Transverse brace
52 Remote radio compass
53 Ventral recognition lights (3)
54 Ventral rod antenna
55 Destructor device
56 Accumulator
57 Radio equipment (lower rack)
58 Entry hand/footholds
59 Engine water injection tank
60 Canopy track
61 Water filler neck
62 Rear-view window
63 Rearward-sliding cockpit canopy (open)

64 Headrest
65 Pilot's head/shoulder armour
66 Canopy sill (reinforced)
67 Fire-extinguisher
68 Oxygen bottle (port fuselage wall)
69 Water tank mounting
70 Underfloor self-sealing fuel tank (60 US gal/ 227 litres)
71 Armoured bulkhead
72 Starboard console
73 Pilot's seat
74 Hydraulic handpump
75 Fuel filler cap and neck

76 Rudder pedals
77 Central console
78 Control column
79 Chart board (horizontal stowage)
80 Instrument panel
81 Panel coaming
82 Reflector gunsight
83 Rear-view mirror
84 Armoured glass windshield
85 Deflection plate (pilot forward protection)

86 Main bulkhead armour-plated upper section with hoisting sling attachments port and starboard)
87 Aluminium alloy aileron trim tab
88 Fabric covered (and taped) aileron surfaces
89 Flush riveted outer wing skin
90 Aluminium alloy sheet wing tip (riveted to wing outer rib)
91 Port navigation (running) light

92 Formed leading-edge (approach/landing light and camera gun inboard)
93 Fixed cowling panel
94 Armour plate (oil tank forward protection)
95 Oil tank (19 US gal/ 72 litres)
96 Welded engine mount fittings
97 Fuselage forward bulkhead
98 Aileron control linkage
99 Engine accessories bay
100 Engine mounting frame (hydraulic fluid reservoir attached to port frames)

101 Controllable cooling gills
102 Cowling ring (removable servicing/ access panels)
103 Pratt & Whitney R-2800-10W twin-row radial air-cooled engine
104 Nose ring profile
105 Reduction gear housing
106 Three-blade Hamilton Standard Hydromatic controllable pitch propeller
107 Propeller hub
108 Engine oil cooler (centre) and supercharger intercooler (outer sections) intakes
109 Oil cooler deflection plate under-protection

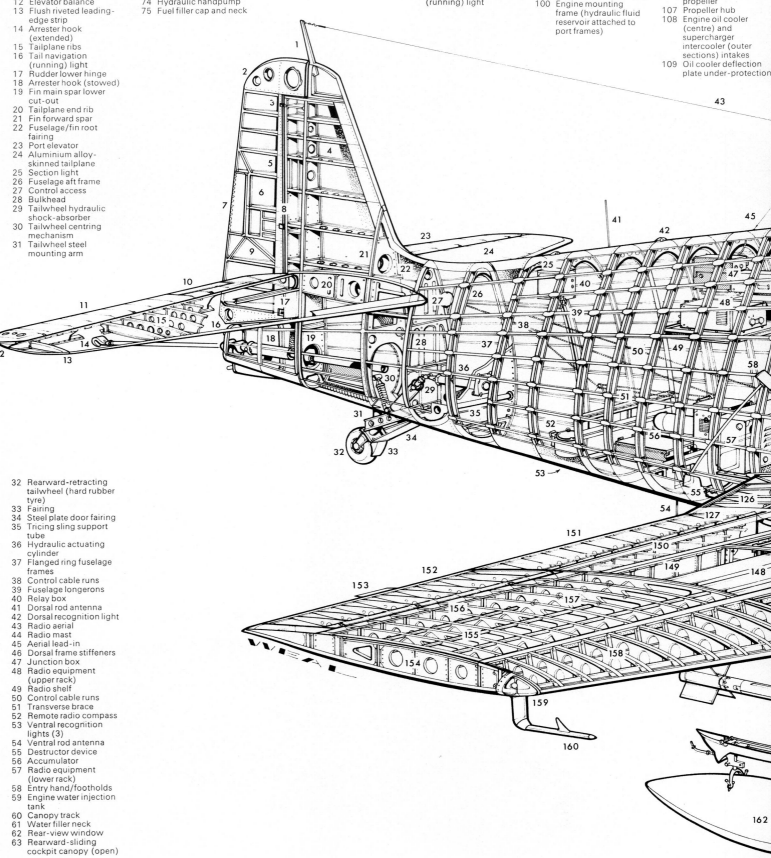

110 Oil cooler duct
111 Intercooler intake duct
112 Mainwheel fairing
113 Port mainwheel
114 Cooler outlet and
    fairing
115 Auxiliary tank support/
    attachment arms
116 Exhaust cluster
117 Supercharger housing
118 Exhaust outlet scoop
119 Wing front spar web
120 Wing front spar/
    fuselage attachment
    bolts
121 Undercarriage
    mounting/pivot point
    on front spar
122 Inter-spar self-sealing
    fuel tanks (port and
    starboard : 87·5 US
    gal/331 litres each)
123 Wing rear spar/
    fuselage attachment
    bolts
124 Structural end rib
125 Slotted wing flap
    profile

126 Wing flap centre-
    section
127 Wing fold line
128 Starboard wheel well
    (doubler-plate
    reinforced edges)
129 Gun bay
130 Removable diagonal
    brace strut
131 Three 0·5-in
    (12·7-mm) Colt
    Browning machine
    guns
132 Auxiliary tank aft
    support
133 Blast tubes
134 Folding wing joint
    (upper surface)
135 Machine-gun barrels
136 Fairing
137 Undercarriage
    actuating strut
138 Mainwheel leg oleo
    hydraulic shock strut
139 Auxiliary tank sling/
    brace
140 Long-range auxiliary
    fuel tank (jettisonable)
141 Mainwheel aluminium
    alloy fairing

142 Forged steel torque
    link
143 Low pressure balloon
    tyre
144 Cast magnesium
    wheel
145 Underwing 5-in
    (12·7 cm)
    air-to-ground RPs
146 Mark V zero-length
    rocket launcher
    installation
147 Canted wing front spar
148 Inter-spar ammunition
    box bay (lower surface
    access)
149 Wing rear spar (normal
    to plane of wing)
150 Rear sub spar
151 Wing flap outer-
    section
152 Frise-type aileron
153 Aileron balance tab

154 Wing outer rib
155 Wing lateral stiffeners
156 Aileron spar
157 Wing outer-section
    ribs
158 Leading-edge rib
    cut-outs
159 Starboard navigation
    (running) light
160 Pitot head
161 Underwing stores
    pylon (mounted on
    fixed centre-section
    inboard of mainwheel
    leg)
162 Auxiliary fuel tank

44

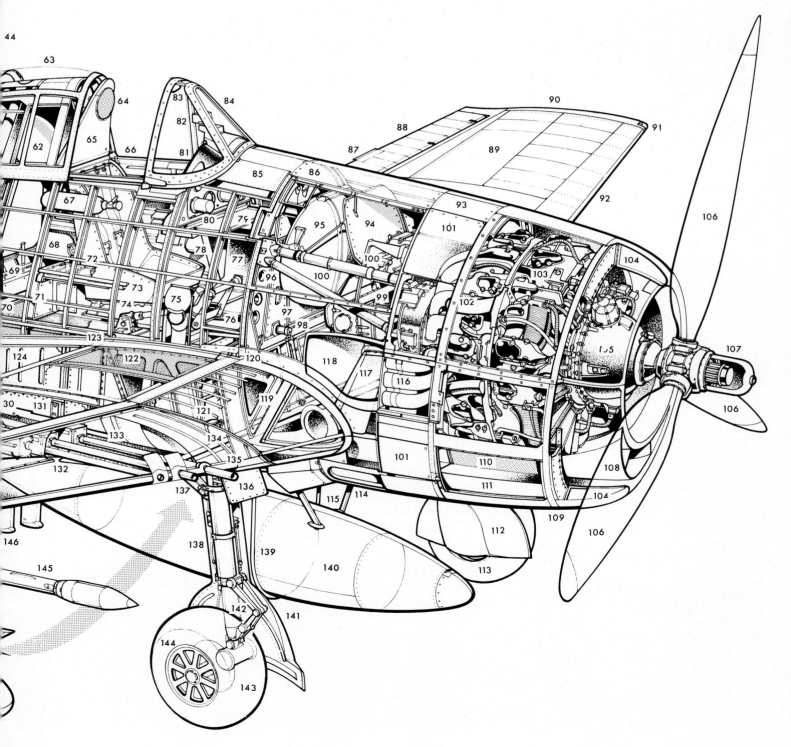

Pacific Pugilists

Hellcat was ready for combat. Within a few months, it was the only fighter embarked on the rapidly growing number of new fast carriers. Cutting edge of the US Navy's sea-air assault forces, it was rugged, reasonably fast, and a stable gunnery platform with a battery of six 0.5-in (12.7-mm) machine-guns. It served as a bomber escort, thereby greatly increasing bomber crew life expectancy. Hellcats established an umbrella of air superiority in the Pacific, and also worked close to the beaches, ploughing paths through Japanese defences with guns, rockets and bombs. It was easily maintained, so it was almost always available. Its overall kill ratio was an astonishing 19:1, a mark out of reach of any other contemporary fighter. Production reached 12,275.

Vought F4U Corsair: delayed by what have always been called 'teething troubles', the Corsair won a 1938 design competition, and first flew on 29 May 1940. It first equipped Marine

Action aboard the fleet carrier USS Enterprise, as Lt Walter Chewning, catapult officer, scrambles up to assist Ensign Byron M. Johnson in the cockpit of the F6F. The left-of-centreline arrival left Johnson almost unharmed, and it only briefly disrupted flying.

An unusual combat picture showing strikes on a 'Zeke' (A6M Zero fighter) by a US Navy F6F on 1 November 1944. The smoke trail behind the F6F comes from the six guns!

Fighting Squadron 124, commissioned 7 September 1942, and sailed early in 1943 for Guadalcanal via Espiritu Santu. The Corsair had great potential which was first realized by the US Marines. They operated the bent-winged birds from dirt strips in the Solomons and the other island chains, swooping down on unsuspecting Japanese outposts. Initially barred from carrier operations because of landing gear bounce, the Corsair finally made it aboard, and proved a fitting team-mate for the Hellcat. Built by both Brewster (although in small quantities as the F3A) and Goodyear (as the FG) as well as Vought, it became the longest-lived of the US Navy's fighters, ending its service career in the Korean War. Like the Hellcat, it was modified to become a night-fighter and a photo-reconnaissance aircraft. Corsairs flew more than 64,000 combat sorties with the US Navy and the US Marines, and about two-thirds of these were logged in the Solomons. Its overall kill ratio was 11:1, and production ceased with the 12,571st

Nothing like so widely famed as the USAAF's Bong, McGuire and Gabreski, or the US Marines' 'Pappy' Boyington, the top-scoring US Navy ace was Commander David S. McCampbell who survived the war with 34 confirmed victories. He gained them all in his F6F after late May 1944!

Night Fighters

At first there was no need for night fighters. Then both main services saw the advantages – and the USAAF procured the mighty Black Widow multi-role aircraft, while the US Navy added small radar sets to its standard fighters.

The classic US World War II night fighter, Northrop's P-61 Black Widow. A pair of P-61C-10s lift off using the 2,800-hp each of their Double Wasp engines.

USAAF no. 44-27234 was one of the P-38Ls converted by field units in the Pacific as two-seat night-fighters in 1944.

Well before America entered the war, observers from the US Army and US Navy had seen how the Germans had bombed London by night during the Blitz Luftwaffe losses were minimal, measured against the results achieved by the bombing, and all the varied means for destroying German aircraft, in combination, hardly posed a serious threat to continuing night operations.

The Americans, impressed with what they had seen, decided that the development of night-fighters was a matter for some priority. The RAF had Bristol Blenheims and Boulton Paul Defiants equipped with airborne interception (AI) radar, tied to ground control of interception (GCI) stations, identification gear to tell friendly aircraft from enemy, radar beacons for navigation and homing in the dark, and VHF radio for communications. Later came Bristol Beaufighters, the hulking aerodynamic beast that had room for radar and a crew to operate it,

Night Fighters

and Douglas DB-7 Havocs, converted from light bombers to night fighters by installing radar in the nose and four cannon in the belly. They had seen enough; the Americans went back home and began to agitate for some dedicated night-fighters.

There were two distinct development trends in those days, one — of course — for each of the major services. The US Army was headed toward the design of a new and large aeroplane. The US Navy needed to adapt its contemporary aircraft to the task; life and logistics were complicated enough aboard carriers without adding to the confusion. But both built on the British experience, learning what they could of tactics and employment of airborne radars.

This olive drab night-fighter was the second of 59 Douglas A-20 attack bombers rebuilt in 1941 as operational trainers with designation P-70. Equipped with British-supplied AI Mk IV radar, they had four cannon in a belly tray, unlike the fully operational P-70A which had 'six fifties' in the nose.

Army night-fighters

It was the US Army's intent to develop a special-purpose fighter for night interception. That service was convinced that heavy, bulky and complex radar had to be carried in a large aircraft, with a multiple-man crew. The pilot would be directed toward the interception by a radarman, and the third man was a defensive gunner. This thinking jelled into a tentative specification which was sent to the Northrop Corporation soon after the initiation of the London Blitz in the late summer of 1940. Northrop turned out a final configuration by 22 November 1940 and submitted it to the USAAC.

A year into the war, the Northrop P-61 (as it was designated) was experiencing troubles, and the USAAF cast about for interim solutions. The first was the Douglas P-70, an 'instant' conversion from a fine light bomber, the A-20G. The USAAF did essentially the same things that the British had done to the DB-7; it was, basically, the same aeroplane, after all. Radar, based on the British design, was added to the nose and a quartet of 20-mm cannon was boxed under the fuselage. In early 1943, P-70s reached service with the 6th Night-Fighter Squadron: Detachment A was based in the Southwest Pacific; Detachment B served on Guadalcanal.

Mid-Pacific improvisation

The P-70 was intended to be a stop-gap solution until the P-61 arrived. But its performance was approximately miserable. It lacked speed, climb and manoeuvrability. So on Guadalcanal, the ingenious mechanics of Detachment B, aided by one of its pilots, began to modify a standard Lockheed P-38. They borrowed a P-70 radar, installed a second seat for its operator, and tested the result. It was no worse than a P-70, and a lot more attractive as an aeroplane.

While this was happening in the Pacific, some USAAF units with the 12th Air Force in North Africa were operating Bristol Beaufighters, taken over from the British in reverse Lend-Lease. Four nightfighter squadrons were so equipped, each with a dozen Beaufighter VIF's carrying British AI Mk VII or Mk VIII, a late-model radar that used centimetric wavelengths. The 'Beau' was never noted for being an exceptionally forgiving aeroplane, and the American units that

flew them experienced an exceptionally high casualty rate. It is likely that the pilots had all come to Beaufighters from tricycle-geared light or medium bombers, and they were unfamiliar with landing the tail-dragger 'Beau'.

The USAAF also experimented with a specially modified two-seat Lockheed P-38, with radar slung in external pods at various locations. It was designated the P-38M when it was finally built, but it was used only for pilot training during World War II.

P-61s began entering combat in the summer of 1944 in the Mediterranean, European and Southwest Pacific theatres. Properly handled, the Black Widow became an effective night fighter and night intruder; its long range and ability to carry as much as 6,400 lb (2903 kg) of bombs made operations officers cast covetous eyes at whatever P-61s were available to fly.

But because it was a first-generation night-fighter, it was quickly outmoded as radar equipment shrank drastically in size and improved markedly in performance. What the Black Widows did in 1944 was duplicated by US Navy night-fighters using far smaller radar equipment tucked into a wing pod.

Army night-fighter sketches

Lockheed P-38M Lightning: its genesis was in 1943 field modifications, to develop a quick stop-gap until delivery of the P-61. Results were inconclusive, although combat tests indicated great potential. The USAAF ordered a prototype P-38L which led to a production order for 75 two-seat P-38M models. Their performance was superior to that of the P-61 in speed, climb, combat radius and ceiling, but the aircraft only reached training units during the war. It was on the verge of combat operations when the war ended.

Development of radar-equipped night-fighters began in the USA in 1940 using British radar technology. The first US night-fighter was the Douglas P-70 with British AI.IV radar, but this did not see active service. Until July 1944, the only night-fighter operational with the USAAF was the Beaufighter VIF, one of which is seen here with the 12th Air Force.

Until July 1944 all front-line night-fighters in the US Army Air Force were British-supplied Beaufighters or Mosquitoes. The most numerous type was the Beaufighter VIF, which equipped Nos 414, 415, 416 (as seen here in Corsica, late 1943) and 417 Sqns, all with the 12th Air Force.

Northrop P-61 Black Widow

The sixth production P-61B became the top-scoring night fighter in the Pacific theatre. It was assigned to the 418th Night Fighter Squadron, based at Hollandia in September 1944.

Night Fighters

Northrop P-61 Black Widow cutaway drawing key

1 Starboard navigation light
2 Starboard formation light
3 Aileron hinge fairing
4 Conventional aileron
5 Aileron tab
6 Full span flaps (Zap type)
7 Retractable aileron (operable as spoiler)
8 Wing skinning
9 De-icer boot
10 Intercooler controllable shutters
11 Intercooler and supercharger induction
12 Fuel filler cap
13 Starboard outer wing fuel tank
14 Nacelle fairing
15 Cooling gills
16 Pratt & Whitney R-2800-65 engine
17 Nacelle ring
18 Starboard outer auxiliary tank
19 Four-bladed Curtiss Electric propeller
20 Propeller cuffs
21 Propeller boss
22 Heater air induction
23 Front spar
24 Plexiglas canopy
25 Cannon access bulkhead cut-out
26 Front gunner's compartment
27 Sighting station
28 Bullet resistant windshield
29 Inter-cockpit/ compartment armour (shaded)
30 Pilot's canopy
31 Pilot's seat
32 Control column
33 Gunsight (fixed cannon)
34 Bullet resistant windshield
35 Fuselage structural joint (armour plate deleted for clarity)
36 Radar modulator
37 Di-electric nose cone
38 SCR-720 Radar scanner
39 Gun camera (gunsight aiming point)
40 Mast
41 Pitot head
42 Radar equipment steel support tube
43 Bulkhead (centre joint)
44 Rudder pedals
45 Drag strut
46 Torque link
47 Towing eye
48 Nosewheel
49 Cantilever steel strut
50 Mudguard (often deleted)
51 Taxi lamp
52 Air-oil shock strut (shimmy damper on forward face)
53 Nosewheel door
54 Cockpit floor
55 Radar aerials
56 Gunner compartment floor (stepped)
57 Forward gunner's seat-swivel mechanism
58 Cannon ports
59 Heater air induction
60 Cannon ammunition magazines
61 Ammunition feed chute
62 20-mm cannon in ventral compartment
63 Magazine forward armour plate
64 Front-spar fuselage cut-out
65 Magazine rear armour plate
66 Rear-spar fuselage cut-out
67 Dorsal turret support/ drive motor
68 Front spar carry-through
59 Turret support forward armour plate
70 Flush-riveted aluminium alloy skin
71 Gun mantlet (four 0.50-in (12.7-mm) machine-guns)
72 General Electric remote-control power turret
73 Turret drive ring
74 Rear spar carry-through
75 Turret support rear armour plate
76 Radio operator/rear gunner's compartment
77 Rear gunner's seat swivel mechanism
78 Plexiglas tail cone
79 Rear compartment glazing
80 Aerial attachment
81 Sighting station
82 Anti-collision beacon
83 Tailboom structure (inner stringers deleted for clarity)
84 Tailboom/fin attachment
85 Tailboom/fin attachment
86 Fin spar attachment (inner face)
87 Rudder lower hinge
88 De-icer boot
89 Fin structure
90 Rudder upper hinge
91 Rudder
92 Rear navigation light
93 Rudder tab
94 Balance tab
95 Horizontal stabilizer structure
96 De-icer boot
97 Trim tab
98 Aerials
99 Elevator
100 De-icer boot
101 Port fin
102 Rudder
103 Rear navigation light
104 Rudder tab
105 Tab hinge fairing
106 Rudder lower hinge
107 Fin spar attachment (outer face)
108 Tailboom/fin attachment butt
109 Tailboom structure
110 Tailboom joint
111 Wing/boom fairing fillet

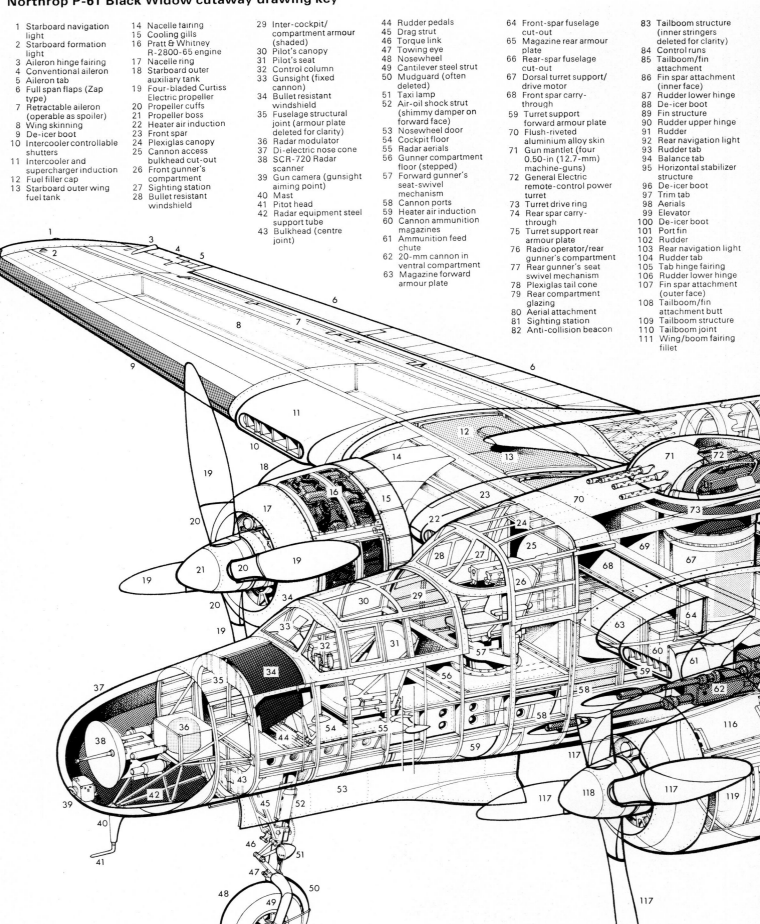

American Fighters of World War II

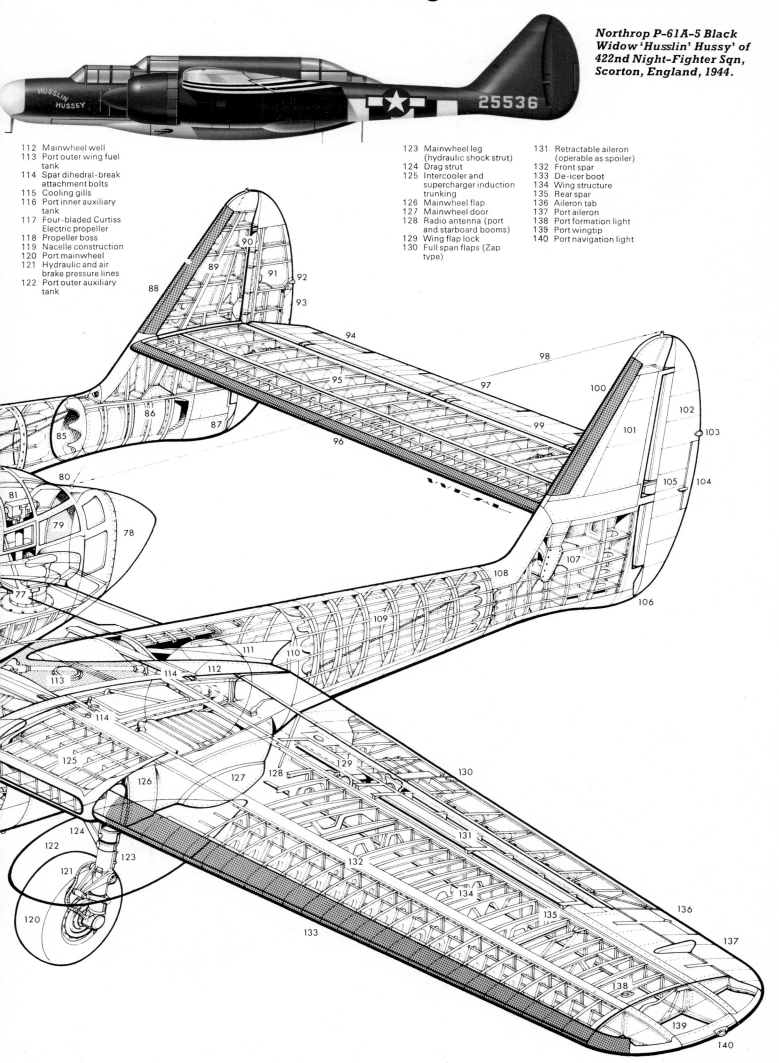

Northrop P-61A-5 Black Widow 'Husslin' Hussy' of 422nd Night-Fighter Sqn, Scorton, England, 1944.

112 Mainwheel well
113 Port outer wing fuel tank
114 Spar dihedral-break attachment bolts
115 Cooling gills
116 Port inner auxiliary tank
117 Four-bladed Curtiss Electric propeller
118 Propeller boss
119 Nacelle construction
120 Port mainwheel
121 Hydraulic and air brake pressure lines
122 Port outer auxiliary tank

123 Mainwheel leg (hydraulic shock strut)
124 Drag strut
125 Intercooler and supercharger induction trunking
126 Mainwheel flap
127 Mainwheel door
128 Radio antenna (port and starboard booms)
129 Wing flap lock
130 Full span flaps (Zap type)

131 Retractable aileron (operable as spoiler)
132 Front spar
133 De-icer boot
134 Wing structure
135 Rear spar
136 Aileron tab
137 Port aileron
138 Port formation light
139 Port wingtip
140 Port navigation light

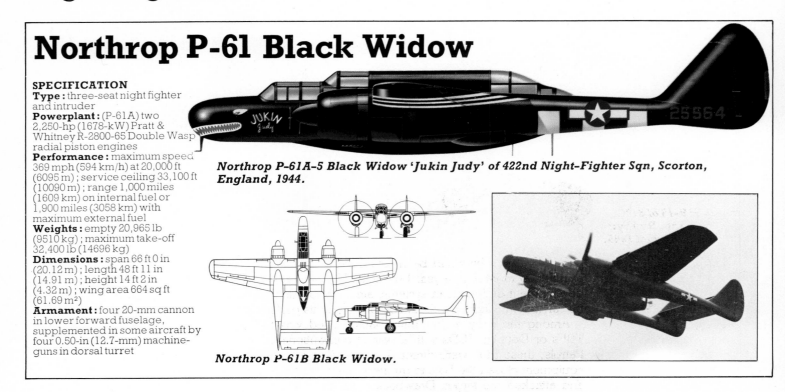

Northrop P-61 Black Widow

SPECIFICATION
Type: three-seat night fighter and intruder
Powerplant: (P-61A) two 2,250-hp (1678-kW) Pratt & Whitney R-2800-65 Double Wasp radial piston engines
Performance: maximum speed 369 mph (594 km/h) at 20,000 ft (6095 m); service ceiling 33,100 ft (10090 m); range 1,000 miles (1609 km) on internal fuel or 1,900 miles (3058 km) with maximum external fuel
Weights: empty 20,965 lb (9510 kg); maximum take-off 32,400 lb (14696 kg)
Dimensions: span 66 ft 0 in (20.12 m); length 48 ft 11 in (14.91 m); height 14 ft 2 in (4.32 m); wing area 664 sq ft (61.69 m²)
Armament: four 20-mm cannon in lower forward fuselage, supplemented in some aircraft by four 0.50-in (12.7-mm) machine-guns in dorsal turret

Northrop P-61A-5 Black Widow 'Jukin Judy' of 422nd Night-Fighter Sqn, Scorton, England, 1944.

Northrop P-61B Black Widow.

Douglas P-70: a desperate attempt to make a night-fighter out of a good low-altitude attack bomber, it did not work. Radar and four 20-mm cannon were added, the aircraft was re-engined, and the performance went to hell. Operational early in 1943 as an interim type pending the arrival of Northrop P-61s, the P-70s themselves required a back-up in the form of field-modified P-38s. The P-70s eventually were used as trainers and, occasionally, as night intruders in the Southwest Pacific.

Northrop P-61 Black Widow: this was the first US aircraft designed specifically for night-fighting. Planned late in 1940, ordered early in 1941, the XP-61 first flew 21 May 1942. Production deliveries began in late 1943, and the Black Widow became operational in early summer 1944. The size of a medium bomber, it weighed twice as much as a loaded P-47. But it was the most manoeuvrable of any US night-fighter, and operated as a very effective night intruder also. Northrop delivered 682 by August 1945, and they cost about $190,000 each.

Navy night-fighters

The US Navy, with its well-established system of shipboard radar detection and fighter direction, extended that system for night operations. Adding short-range radar equipment to standard fighters provided 'fine-tuning' of the ship's control and enabled fighters to close to lethal gunnery range.

Big, powerful and extremely complicated, the Northrop P-61 Black Widow was the first aircraft designed from scratch as a radar-equipped night-fighter. This trio are from the 9th Air Force's 422nd Night-Fighter Sqn, based at Scorton and heading out over France after D-Day.

American Fighters of World War II

Northrop P-61A-1 Black Widow 'Jap Batty' of 6th Night-Fighter Sqn, Saipan, 1944.

Northrop P-61B-15 of 548th Night-Fighter Sqn, Ryukyu Islands, Japan, August 1945.

25528

Close relationships had been established with the British, and radar information was actively exchanged more than a year before the US went to war. British AI equipment was the basis for development of American systems, aimed at producing a small and lightweight unit that could be carried on a fighter without compromising its performance.

Among the early night-fighting tactics used was the teaming of radar-equipped Grumman TBFs or Douglas SBDs with a pair of conventional fighters flown by skilled pilots. Called 'Bat Patrols', these trios were directed toward targets located by their carrier's radar. The airborne equipment closed the Bats to gunnery range, and one of the two fighters made a visual sighting and attacked the target. Drawbacks of such a system were obvious. Team co-ordination was difficult, and depended of the rapid passing of accurate information among aircraft. Further, dependence on visual sighting was, at best, a weak reed on which to lean the whole offensive attack.

The first US Navy dedicated night-fighter squadron—VF (N)-75—began operating in October 1943 out of Munda, New Georgia, halfway up the Solomon Islands chain. On October 31, the squadron—flying Vought F4U-2 aircraft with AIA (Airborne Intercept radar type A)—logged its first night-time kill.

During the first half of 1944, the US Navy sent three more night-fighter squadrons to the Pacific and based them, in detachments, on nine carriers. Each detachment had a mixed complement of F6F-3E and F6F-3N Hellcats. The former carried search radar, and the latter carried the interception radar. The planes worked as a team of one -3E and one -3N.

But the US Navy found, in its early experimentation with night-fighting and radar, that it was hardly worth the trouble. Flying off carriers in those days involved much respotting of aircraft. The night-fighters had to be moved from the flight deck parking area, or up from the hangar deck, and room had to be made for their launch and recovery. The results obtained by the fighters were not, in many eyes, justifying the effort.

A dedicated night-fighter group was attached to the light carrier USS Independence from September 1944 until January 1945. Air Group 41 pioneered tactics and information processing that later became the foundation of the US Navy's night-fighter work. It marked the high point of

After the first 37, the Northrop P-61A did not have the dorsal turret, which when fitted added four 0.5-in (12.7-mm) guns each with 560 rounds, to back up the already heavy punch of four 20-mm cannon with 200 rounds apiece in the belly. This P-61A-10 is parked at Scorton immediately on delivery on 2 June 1944.

Night Fighters

Fully developed in time for the Korean war, the F4U–5N was a 1948 night fighter with four 20-mm cannon, radar and rocket launchers. Here a production –5N is seen on factory test over the Connecticut shore.

the US Navy's wartime night-fighting effort. Six-plane detachments (generally four F6F-5N and two F6F-5E aircraft) served on board most of the carriers until the end of the war. But their kill record was not at all comparable with that of the daytime fighters.

Perhaps the brightest spot for the US Navy effort was the request from General Douglas MacArthur's headquarters. A US Marine night-fighter squadron — VMF (N)-541 — was requested to replace the P-61s on Tacloban early in December 1944. The P-61s were not able to do the missions that MacArthur's air operations staff required, and the US Marines' night-fighter Corsairs were. But they found to their disgust that they spent most of the time flying combat air patrols at dawn and dusk, rather than fighting at night. Nevertheless, they did what they were ordered to do, and became the only US Marine air unit to receive an Army Distinguished Unit Citation during the war.

Grumman delivered 1,434 F6F-5N night fighters as well as 80 similar Hellcat NF. IIs for the Fleet Air Arm. These very useful machines are seen here aboard a US escort carrier in the final year of the war.

Powered by two Double Wasp engines of over 2,000 hp each, the F7F-3N Tigercat was potentially a great fighter. This F7F-3N was a two-seat radar-equipped version of 1945 used by the Marines from shore bases.

Navy night-fighter sketches

Both the Grumman Hellcat and the Vought Corsair were produced in quantity in night-fighter models. The modification placed the radar equipment in a streamlined pod built into the outboard leading edge of the starboard wing. Performance was not greatly affected by the additional drag, although the stall could be a little tricky with that aerodynamic trigger sticking out in front of the wing. Early models of both aircraft carried the AN/APS-4 airborne search radar; later models were equipped with AN/APS-6 airborne intercept radars of improved performance. Both aircraft often had new armament, a quartet of 20-mm cannon replacing the six 0.5-in (12.7-mm) machine-guns that were the standard battery.

The US Navy pioneered the use of miniaturized radars working on a wavelength of 3 cm for installation in single-seaters. This Grumman F6F-5N not only has the APS-6 pod on its right wing but two 20-mm cannon, with flash eliminators, plus four 0.5-in (12.7-mm) guns and six zero-length rocket attachments.

Non-Contenders

With fine aircraft in production, little thought was given to experimental types. But the aero industry itself came up with some weird and wonderful prototypes, and then the jet engine led to massive new programmes.

The wartime environment bred new designs as well as special modifications. But none of the aircraft that entered development during World War II moved rapidly enough to serve in a combat theatre before the Japanese surrender. Several did survive the decimating cuts in production after VJ-Day, to become mainstays of the post-war fighter strength of both the US Army Air Forces and the US Navy. Let us look at the aircraft that first flew during the war years, and see what prompted them and what happened to them.

The Bell P-63 Kingcobra began as an improved P-39, redesigned around the new NACA laminar-flow wing, the basic aerofoil section used for the NAA Mustang, and with a new Continental engine intended to replace the Allison. The wings were tested on three modified P-39Ds, results justified a go-ahead, and two prototype XP-63 aircraft were ordered on 27 June 1941. The first flew on 7 December 1942; production had been ordered the previous September, and deliveries began in October 1943. The plane was rugged, with great firepower,

Designed with great rapidity around two General Electric 1-A (Whittle) turbojets, the Bell P-59A Airacomet was the USA's first jet.

and unwanted by the USAAF, who saw to it that 2,421 out of the total production of 3,303 went to the Russians. An additional 300 went to the Free French. The rest were converted to flying pin-ball machines, target aircraft with heavy armour, fired at by bomber gunners in training, using frangible bullets. Would you bet that the USAAF really did not want the job of ground support, which was what the P-63 was best fitted to do.

When the USAAF finally woke up to the crying need for escorts for its bomber fleets, a requirement surfaced in January 1944. The USAAF was still smarting from two disastrous raids on Schweinfurt the previous August and October, which consumed more than 25 per cent of the attacking bombers and, more importantly, their crews. North American Aviation proposed tying two Mustangs together for the job, and showed the USAAF the first drawings of the

Though a reasonably adequate fighter, the P-63 Kingcobra was never used in numbers by the US forces and almost all the 3,303 production machines went to America's allies. The Soviet Union received 2,421, where they proved the most popular and intensively used of all US combat machines supplied to that country. This was the sixth production aircraft.

Had it been designed in parallel with the P-51 in 1940 the P-82 Twin Mustang would have made a notable contribution to Allied victory. As it was only a modest number (270) were built, almost all post-war and with Allison engines.

Non-Contenders

XP-82 Twin Mustang on 7 January 1944. The USAAF ordered three prototypes and 500 production aircraft. The first prototype flew 6 July 1945, but the order was cut back drastically at war's end. Eventually, the Twin Mustang was used as a bomber escort and a night fighter. It got the first kill in the Korean conflict, where it saw limited combat action.

Too late the Tigercat

The US Navy had a new class of carrier coming, the 45,000-ton USS *Midway* and her sister ships, and wanted a long-range, twin-engined fighter to operate from them. Grumman developed one of the most elegant piston-engined aircraft ever seen by human eyes. The XF7F-1 Tigercat prototype made its first test flight on 2 December 1943, but it was later declared unsuitable for carrier use. Give it to the US Marines, said the US Navy, and after 35 had been built, production switched to a night-fighter version. There were brief carrier trials of the new type in April 1945 aboard the USS *Antietam*, and VMF (N)-533 took its new Tigercats

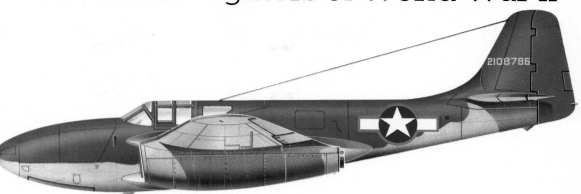

to the Pacific, arriving on Okinawa the day before the Japanese surrender.

In autumn 1943, the US Navy needed a fast-climbing interceptor with limited range. Grumman started the design of the XF8F-1 Bearcat, a potent package of power. Two prototypes were ordered 27 November 1943, and the first flew on 21 August 1944. By October, Grumman was sure it had a winner; a production order for 2,023 had come through, and Eastern Aircraft soon after received another whopping order. The first US Navy acceptance of a production Bearcat took place in February 1945, and by May F8F-1s were being delivered to Navy Fighting Squadron (VF) 19. The unit was working up for combat deployment aboard the USS *Boxer* when the war ended.

Enter the jet age

The greatest influence of the war years was jet propulsion. Germany flew a prototype fighter 27 August 1939; the British duplicated the feat 15 May 1941. On 5 September, the USAAF told Bell Aircraft Corporation to design a fighter around General Electric jet engines and to build three prototypes. Construction began in early January 1942, and the first XP-59 Airacomet was shipped by rail to a remote airfield at Muroc, California (now part of the vast Edwards AFB complex). It flew 1 October 1942, but only 15 flight hours were logged in the first five months. Thirteen service-test Airacomets were built, and a couple were evaluated in mock combat against a P-47D and a P-38J. The new jet was, disappointingly, outclassed by the planes it was supposed to replace. The USAAF suggested that the P-59 be used for research and training. Fifteen went to the 412th Fighter Group at Bakersfield, California, the first USAAF jet unit. The value of the entire project was that it provided a cadre of jet pilots for the US Air Force.

A new Lockheed pursuit, first built around a British jet engine, was begun in May 1943 and

Above: *Most powerful carrier-based aircraft of its day, the Grumman XF7F-1 was the prototype of what became the F7F Tigercat, flying in December 1943. Production F7F-1s entered service with land-based US Marine units from October 1944 and combined great performance with devastating firepower.*

Though it looked stumpy and unstreamlined, the Grumman F8F Bearcat was not only a most agile fighter but also a tremendous performer, a racing version later gaining the world's piston-engined speed record at almost 500 mph (805 km/h).

American Fighters of World War II

By far the best US fighter flown during World War II, the Lockheed P-80 Shooting Star was too late to see action. This particular example was the 13th of 345 production P-80As, larger than the XP-80 and powered by the J33-GE-9 engine.

first flew on 8 January 1944, a remarkable accomplishment. Thirteen re-engined P-80 Shooting Stars entered service testing, which included four sent to the European and Mediterranean theatres of war, where they served until VE-Day. In January 1945, the USAAF assigned the P-80 programme the highest priority, placing it on a level with the Boeing B-29. By mid-1945, the 412th was re-equipping with Shooting Stars. The war ended before they got into action. But the P-80 became the foundation of the USAAF post-war fighter fleet, fought in the Korean conflict with distinction, and is still today—nearly 40 years after its design—still in active duty with the USAF.

McDonnell Aircraft Corporation was asked to do the same thing for the US Navy in early 1943, but the design was tied to Westinghouse jet engines, powerplants that never lived up to their promise. It was the US Navy's first jet; almost two years elapsed between first drawings and first flight on 26 January 1945. Too late for the war, the type served aboard post-war carriers as the FD-1. To avoid confusion with Douglas products, it was redesignated FH-1 and

The first McDonnell jet, and the first jet designed to operate from aircraft carriers, the XFD-1 flew in January 1945. The St Louis company later delivered 60 production machines, redesignated FH-1 to avoid confusion with Douglas.

Non-Contenders

This gaily painted Shooting Star was the 236th P-80A-1, serving in 1946 with the 412th Fighter Group. All P-80A-1s had a highly polished grey paint finish which was intended to reduce drag.

called the Phantom. Its descendant, the F-4 Phantom II, is a primary USAF and USN/USMC fighter today.

The US Navy, hedging its bets, had ordered a mixed powerplant fighter, the Ryan FR-1 Fireball, in February 1943. It had a piston engine in the nose, and a single jet in the tail. It first flew 25 June 1944, and production deliveries began in January 1945. First **squadron** deliveries were made in March 1945, and VF-66 became carrier-qualified in the plane on 1 May 1945. The war ended with the Ryan still unblooded, and they were withdrawn from service after jets proved their worth.

Non-runnners

An even dozen prototypes of other, sometimes even more exotic, USAAF pursuits flew during the war years (first flight date in parentheses):

Lockheed XP-49 (11 November 1942) was an enlarged and re-engined P-38, but without better performance

Vultee XP-54 (15 January 1943) was a twin-boomed pusher bearing an obscene nickname; it was intended as an interceptor, then as a bomber destroyer, neither of which roles was achieved

Curtiss XP-55 (13 July 1943) was called the Ascender because it looked as if it flew tail-first. It had many real problems

Northrop XP-56 Black Bullet (30 September 1943) was a tiny flying wing; it looked great, but flew poorly

Lockheed XP-58 Chain Lightning (6 June 1944) was a monstrous P-38; AAF never decided on an appropriate mission

Curtiss XP-62 (May 1943) was intended a competitor to the Republic P-47 ; it was not

One of numerous unconventional wartime fighter prototypes was the Curtiss XP-55 Ascender. Three were built, with Allison engines and four 0.5-in (12.7-mm) guns, but they were markedly inferior to the P-51.

Unofficially called the Black Bullet, the Northrop XP-56 was a bold attempt to get the highest possible performance. Powered by a Double Wasp, replacing the more powerful P&W X-1800, it was made mainly of magnesium.

McDonnell XP-67 (6 January 1944) was an aerodynamic dream lost to a ground fire and cancelled

Republic XP-72 (2 February 1944) was a hulking P-47 with twice the engine power and contra-rotating propellers; then the USAAF changed the requirements

Fisher XP-75 Eagle (17 November 1943) was an intended interceptor assembled, at first, from parts of other aircraft; like a horse designed by a committee, this was also a camel

Bell XP-77 (1 April 1944) was a tiny all-wood fighter intended to manoeuvre with the Zeroes; there were not many Zeroes left by the time it flew

Vultee XP-81 (7 February 1945) was another composite powerplant design, intended for bomber escort; it was too late

Bell XP-83 (25 February 1945) was an overblown P-59 with inherited characteristics.

The first prototype Fisher (General Motors) XP-75 long-range escort had an Allison V-3420 double engine amidships, an SBD tail, F4U landing gears and P-40 outer wings. The production P-75 was redesigned as an uncompromised design, but only five were completed, 2,495 being cancelled.

Non-Contenders

The US Navy, being somewhat more conservative, had fewer of these non-contenders. They flew the big Boeing XF8B-1 on 27 November 1944, after which Boeing sensibly stayed with transport and bomber design. The Curtiss XF14C-2, a second attempt to get a design right, flew in July 1944. The Curtiss XF15C-1 was a jet fighter design with a T-tail; it had good flying characteristics, according to reports, but was too late for the war and became outmoded very soon after by developments.

And there they are, the good, the bad and the indifferent, the American fighters of World War II. There were two or three great ones, another half dozen that were not bad and fought well, and a small galaxy of failures. The pattern was the same for every other belligerent's designs. We celebrate today the Spitfire and the Hurricane, the Bf 109 and the Fw 190, the Mustang, Hellcat, Thunderbolt and Lightning. Eight, out of dozens. It's a tough world, and only the fittest survive.

TERESA BATEMAN

THE MERBABY

PATIENCE BREWSTER
ILLUSTRATIONS

Holiday House / New York

Library of Congress Cataloging-in-Publication Data
Batemen, Teresa.
The merbaby / by Teresa Bateman; illustrated by Patience Brewster—1st ed.
p. cm.
Summary: When he and his brother, Josh, find a merbaby
caught in their fishing net, Tarron, rejecting his brother's plan to sell the baby
and make a profit, discovers that there are greater treasures than gold.
ISBN 0-8234-1531-7 (hardcover)
[1. Mermaids—Fiction. 2. Brothers—Fiction. 3. Fishers—Fiction.
4. Conduct of life—Fiction.] I. Brewster, Patience, ill. II Title.
PZ7.B294435 Me 2001
[E]—dc21   00-035097

In loving memory
of my brother, Tony—
the first of us to sail
beyond the horizon
T. B.

To Marietta,
the beautiful merbaby
I got to hold
for a *while*
P. B.

"**M**ind what you're doing, Tarron!"
Josh shouted from the helm, half hidden
in fog. "Take your head out of the clouds and
look to the sea—that's where your fortune lies!"

Tarron looked at the net in his hands, feeling like
a prisoner. He loved the sea, but he didn't love fishing.

His brother, Josh, viewed the sea as a treasure chest of
silver-scaled jewels waiting to be plucked for a profit. He was
forever talking of that one great catch that would set them up
for life.

It was his brother who had insisted they come here, to dangerous waters shunned by other fishermen. Josh said the fishing was rich enough to be worth the risk.

Tarron sighed. Truth be told, he wanted the money, too, though for a different reason. He hoped one day to buy his own ship and become his own master. Then he could follow the stars as they turned above him. Trade and travel, exploration and excitement—those were the things he longed for.

Now there were fish to be tipped into the hold, sails to raise or lower, and nets to be mended. It was a hard life, and Josh was a hard taskmaster. Tarron saw long years ahead of cold fish and scaly decks. Only the dream of his own ship kept him going.

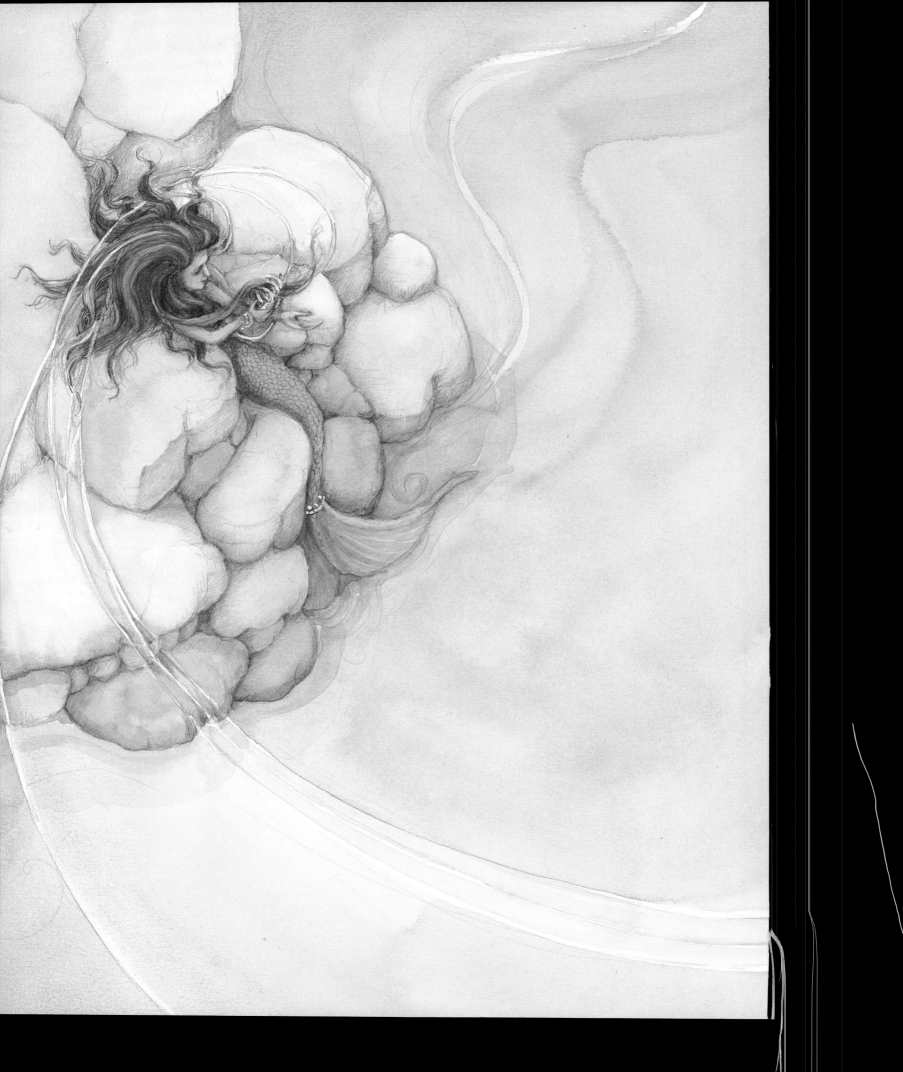

Because the dream filled his thoughts, Tarron did not at first hear the song weaving its way through the wind, but Josh heard it. The ship seemed pulled, and they tacked suddenly starboard.

Tarron glanced up. His brother's eyes were dull and glazed. Then Tarron heard it, too: a melody like a beckoning finger. He was alert enough to wrap his muffler tightly around his ears and leap for the wheel, swinging hard aport.

Ahead, a tiny island of solitary rocks jutted upward. A beautiful figure sat there, combing her hair with a fish's skeleton—singing them to their doom.

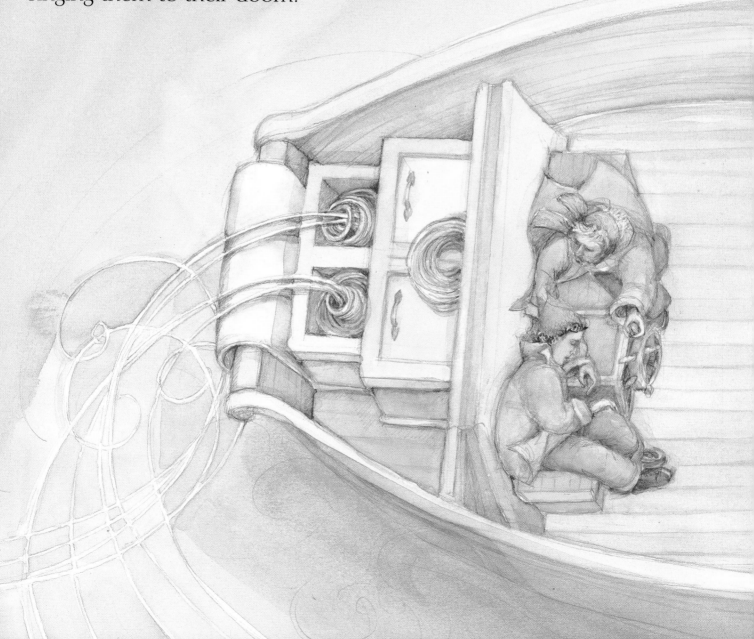

The mermaid's song faltered as she saw the ship veer. She raised angry eyes to Tarron's. He could barely tear his own eyes away. Then the sails caught the wind. As they turned, he imagined he could feel rocks scraping barnacles from the hull.

Many long minutes passed before the rock vanished in the fog and Tarron dared uncover his ears. He watched his brother blink and awaken from his daze.

Josh did not at first believe Tarron's tale. When convinced, however, he turned on his brother angrily. "How often have I said that you must take what the sea offers? Why didn't you seize the chance and capture the mermaid? She would have been both our fortune and our fame."

Tarron's shoulders slumped. Surely his brother was wrong. Still, that night in his hammock, he thought of the wealth—and the ship—that might have been his if, indeed, he had captured the mermaid.

It was the next day that the nets hauled in an unexpected treasure. Tarron saw it first, blinked, then looked again. A baby's face peered out from among the fish. Tarron scanned the horizon for ships, but there was none to be seen. Yet, there in the net gurgled a small smiling face topped by golden curls.

Tarron lifted the child into his arms, only then seeing a fish's tail where dimpled legs should have been. He had never heard of such a thing as a merbaby, yet that was surely what he held in his arms. Tarron's first impulse was to return the child to the sea. Looking over the side, however, he saw shark fins slicing the water below.

A small hand patted his cheek,
and he looked into sea green eyes
as plump arms circled his neck. A
seashell necklace with the name
Meri written in gold pressed against
him, identifying the child as a girl.
Then Josh caught sight of Tarron's
"catch." "Good work!" he exclaimed,
clapping Tarron on the back. "We
can sell it, or put it in a glass cage
and charge admission. Our fortune
is made!"

Tarron glowed. For once he was not only accepted but admired. He also knew that the fortune his brother spoke of would mean his own freedom.

It wasn't until that night, as he lay in his hammock and heard the gentle splash of the merbaby in a washtub of seawater nearby, that doubts bubbled up in his mind. He fell asleep at last. In his dreams he saw the merbaby brought into port to be stared at by uncaring gawkers. He heard the clink of the coins he and his brother would earn and, beneath it, the soft sobbing of the merbaby trapped in a glass cage, never to know the sea again.

Tarron awoke in a cold sweat after only an hour of troubled sleep and knew he couldn't do it: he couldn't buy his own happiness at the expense of another's.

It was true that merfolk sought only the death of those born on the land, calling them to their doom with siren songs. Yet, would landfolk act differently if their shores were invaded by strangers taking whatever they wished? The hatred between the two groups was long-standing. Still, Tarron could not forget the feel of Meri's trusting arms curled around his neck.

"I'm a fool," Tarron admitted, but he knew what he had to do. He could no more take this merchild onto land than he could throw a human child into the sea. Nor would he toss Meri overboard, like a too-small fish, into strange waters far from her home. He needed to entrust her to another of her kind, and there was only one whose location was sure in his mind. He tried not to think of the danger.

Tarron smiled into the washtub, then strode on deck. "I can't sleep," he said to Josh. "I thought I'd do the night watch, since I'm awake."

Josh smiled. "All the more time for me to dream of coming riches."

When snores filled the night air, Tarron gently twisted the wheel, returning them eastward. The ship swiftly swallowed the miles before it.

It was nearly dawn when Tarron knew he had to leave the ship behind. It would not be fair to risk his brother's life as well as his own. He tiptoed into the cabin and carefully lifted the washtub with the merbaby. Saltwater soaked his feet as he carried the tub to the ship's dingy. He threw a few supplies into the boat, then lowered it.

Tarron turned the ship west again, lashing the wheel in place. Then he tucked a candle in his pocket and slid down a rope to the dingy below, where Meri greeted him with a smile and a splash.

He rowed east as the ship sailed west. They surged across the waves, stopping only at noon to eat and for Tarron to make a tent of his jacket over the washtub.

The sun was halfway to the horizon when he heard the first wisps of a song settling across the sea like a fishing net. Quickly Tarron dug the warm candle from his pocket, molding the wax off the wick into two plugs that he placed carefully in his ears. Suddenly the world became eerily still. Waves moved soundlessly in a silent sea. Ahead he caught a glimpse of stones. He rowed on, glancing over his shoulder as the jagged rocks grew to fill his horizon.

Then he saw her: the mermaid, her lips moving in song and her eyes dark with mystery. He shipped the oars as the boat neared the rocks, letting it drift in.

The mermaid's lips stilled, and her eyes were wide in amazement, pinned to the merbaby in the washtub. Tarron scooped Meri out of the water, giving her a gentle kiss before placing her in the mermaid's arms. "Can you find her family?" he asked, the words echoing strangely behind stopped-up ears.

The mermaid nodded silently, solemnly. Then she gave a cry he could not hear.

Tarron took up his oars again and made to row away from the rocks. The boat, however, refused to move. Tarron looked over his shoulder to discover he was surrounded by merfolk. He wasn't going anywhere.

Did they think he had kidnapped the child? If so, they would exact their revenge. Still, he could not regret what he had done.

The mermaid motioned to Tarron's ears. Since he was already their prisoner, he removed the wax. Her voice was musical as she spoke, yet Tarron felt none of the compulsion of her song. "Come."

Tarron scrambled up to the mermaid. He stood beside her and scanned the sea. It was alive with bobbing heads focused on the rocks. Tarron felt like a condemned prisoner facing execution.

The mermaid spoke again, and her voice rang over the waves. "What was lost has been found. What was taken has been returned. Let us do the same."

There was a sheen of silver as a thousand tails flicked the sea.

Soon they were back, carrying treasures from ships that had met their doom in merfolk waters: pearl necklaces, gold coins, jewels of all kinds. These were placed into Tarron's small boat until it nearly sank from the weight.

"I didn't return Meri for a reward," he protested.

"All the more reason you should have one," the mermaid replied. "You risked all to return her. We never thought to see such courage or kindness from a land-man. From this time forth you shall be called mer-friend, and will always find a welcome in our waters."

He bowed awkwardly to the mermaid, let Meri grasp his finger one last time, then scrambled down the rocks again.

Cautiously stepping into the well-laden boat, Tarron dug the oars out. He knew he couldn't make it safely to land with so much weight in the boat. He began to edge away gently, thinking he'd lighten his load when out of sight of his new friends.

He had underestimated them, however. As soon as he was away from the rocks, the boat was surrounded by a vast school of fish that caught the wooden vessel up on their myriad backs and carried him swiftly away, leaving only when he was in sight of port.

Tarron shared his fortune with his brother, then purchased a smart ship with crisp white sails. He returned from each voyage with rare treasures and fantastic tales.

Still, through
all the years,
the treasure
he always held
closest to his heart
was the memory
of the merbaby's
smile.

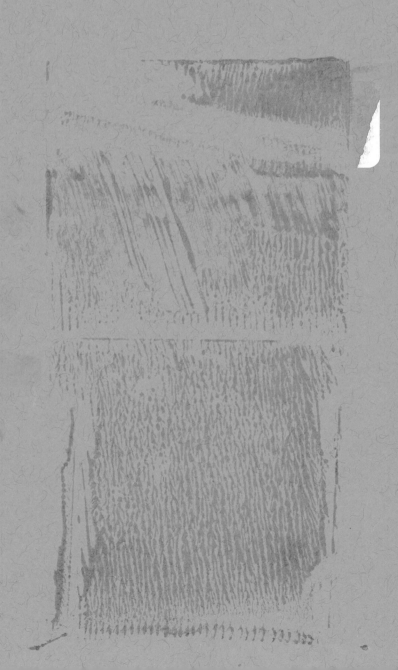